Table of Contents

Introduction

Teachers are under the microscope as parents and politicians demand accountability and student success. All agree that for our country to continue to be successful, its citizens must be literate. Everyone seems to have an opinion about the best way to accomplish literacy for all. Although this debate continues, there is a great deal that is known about what a good reader does and the skills and strategies a child must learn to become a good reader.

It is critical that children receive the most knowledgeable and effective literacy teaching because students who are not independent readers by the end of third grade are handicapped (Stanovich, 1986). Dependent readers are not motivated to practice something they struggle with and find difficult to enjoy. As a result, they do not mature as readers.

Reading can be thought of as a complex behavior whereby the child constructs his or her own understanding about how print works to convey meaning. With scaffolding or using what a child already knows or can control, the child is "guided" to become an independent reader. The guidance ensures that the child develops strategies and the necessary skills to read without assistance.

...what now needs to be explained is what it is about reading and writing that helps the good reader to become better as a result of his own efforts. Something about the ways in which they read creates a forward thrust, and perhaps this is something that poor readers have not managed to learn. To formulate the question in a different way we could ask what is the generating power controlled by the independent reader that gives him or her such easy access to quantities of reading, and what processes does that reader need to control to get a rapid expansion of vocabulary? (Clay, 1991, p. 4).

A teacher makes hundreds of decisions that affect learning. To make good decisions, the teacher must have a thorough understanding of what students need to learn, how to analyze the students' strengths, and how to correct any misunderstandings students have.

Teachers need scaffolding, too. Teachers come to teaching with different backgrounds and understandings. This books attempts to provide guidance that supports the implementation of a successful and effective balanced program utilizing guided reading. It describes guided reading. It then outlines the steps for starting a guided reading program and includes specific examples for assessing students, grouping for instruction, planning guided reading lessons, setting up the various components of a balanced program, and using literacy centers. It addresses materials as well as ways to level and organize books.

The challenge and responsibility of teaching children to read is enormous. Hopefully, this book will lighten the load and give teachers the assistance necessary to enjoy and appreciate this critical and rewarding time in a child's life.

Guided Reading in a Balanced Program

Evangelyn Visser
Gary M. Hanggi, M.A.

Teacher Created Materials, Inc.

Cover Design by Darlene Spivak

Made in U.S.A.

ISBN 1-57690-477-6

Order Number TCM 2477

www.teachercreated.com

An Effective Reading Program

How do people learn how to read? First, they must be motivated to learn. This includes being willing to work at it. They must acquire specific skills that make print accessible. Finally, they must create a workable set of strategies to deal with texts that present new difficulties. The goal is to want and be able to read unfamiliar texts.

It would be wonderful to have a reading approach that ensured that each child learned to read. However, children are different and come to the task with different backgrounds and understandings.

Many people talk about reading readiness, especially in kindergarten and first grade. Children who are ready to read and write have four critical understandings.

1. *They know that ideas and words can be written down.*

2. *They know that when you read or write there is a story or some information that you are trying to understand or communicate.*

3. *They know that reading and writing are two important things that bigger people do and since they want to be big too, they must learn.*

4. *They know from overwhelming adult pleasure and approval of their fledgling attempts at pretend reading, or their reading of some signs and labels, and of their writing that they are succeeding at mastering this mysterious code (Cunningham and Allington, 1999, p. 24).*

The goal is to want and be able to read unfamiliar texts.

When a child comes to school without these understandings, the first thing the school must do is to foster these understandings—because for whatever reason, the child is not going acquire them up from his or her home.

In addition, research (Dole, Duffy, Roehler, and Pearson, 1991; Johnston and Allington, 1991) clearly demonstrates that at-risk children make more rapid progress when given explicit instruction in how to read and write. So it is important that the approach used to teach reading is effective, regardless of learning style or prior knowledge.

A Balanced Program

Cunningham and Allington (1999) feel that one logical way to achieve balance is to include a variety of instructional approaches. They recognize four basic approaches.

Systematic, Explicit Phonics

The phonetic approach starts with the premise that written English is an alphabetic language. In other words, the letters in a written word stand for the sounds made when the word is said. To read, all that is required is to learn which letters stand for which sounds.

Unfortunately, spoken English has changed over time and spelling has not. This has led to words that cannot be sounded out, i.e., are not decodeable. In fact, of the 150 most frequent words in schoolbook English, only 35 can be decoded (Adams, 1990), e.g., *the, of, a, to, you* are not decodeable; *and, in, is, it* are. In addition, many foreign words and morphemes, especially Latin, Greek, and French, have been added to the language. Many of these words retain their foreign spelling which leads to exceptions in spelling and pronunciation.

Basal

To deal with the problems caused by the fact that many of the most common words are not decodeable, reading approaches were developed that emphasized sight words. These approaches generally used repetition to help the student memorize words. This is the whole-word method found in older basal series such as Scott Foresman's Dick and Jane series.

Some basal series include phonics, some more systematically than others. The vocabulary of the reading selections is carefully controlled; the level of difficulty is gradually increased. The role of the teacher is spelled out in the teacher's edition, which emphasizes teacher-guided reading. There are usually work sheets that can be used to keep busy children who are not reading with the teacher.

Individualized

A controlled vocabulary can result in stilted text that does not "sound" right to the student and may result in uninteresting stories. This led to the development of an individualized reading approach popularized by Jean Veatch (1959). This approach promotes individual selection of trade books.

In theory, students select books they are motivated to read. The teacher's role is to confer with each reader individually and provide whatever help is required. This approach also led to reading series that contained trade books. This approach has also been incorporated in the whole-language movement. It is sometimes called reading workshop.

Language Experience

The fourth approach states that to understand the alphabetic principle,

The phonetic approach starts with the premise that written English is an alphabetic language.

children need to see speech put into print. Stories are generated from a shared student experience. The children watch as their speech is mapped onto the letters that are used to produce the text, they have a personal interest in the story and they are then given the text to practice reading.

For example, the children make peanut butter and jelly sandwiches. The teacher and children then write on chart paper what they did. The teacher may print additional copies of this story for the children to read, add to the class library, or take home to read to parents.

Learning Styles and Reading Approaches

Each of these methods has benefits and, as Cunningham and Allington (1994) point out, appeals to different personalities or learning styles. Some children are fascinated with the sounds of language. They can hear the sounds in words (phonemic awareness) before they enter school. For them, seeing how the sounds relate to letter(s) may be all they need to figure out how to make sense of print.

Finally, children with their own ideas and vivid imaginations would much rather read their own stories than those of another author.

The basal approach is very structured. This approach appeals to children who prefer to have clear boundaries between right and wrong, who are uncomfortable with open-ended projects.

Some children are able to quickly figure out how things work, including how language is written down. They need the freedom to explore their own interests and choose appropriate responses and activities to accompany their reading and writing. These children blossom with an individualized approach.

Finally, children with their own ideas and vivid imaginations would often rather read their own stories than those of another author. Language experience appeals to them.

While it is not possible to clearly determine which children will learn best with what approach, it is clear when a teacher provides more routes to the goal of literacy, more children will find a route to take them there (Cunningham and Allington, 1999, p. 16).

Setting Up a Balanced Program

Cunningham advocates a four block approach to balance literacy learning (Cunningham, Hall, Defee, 1998). The four blocks are each about 30 to 40 minutes long and include Word Work, Guided Reading, Writing Workshop, and Independent Reading.

Word Work

Word Work provides strong phonics instruction as well as working with high-frequency sight words. It includes activities such as

Making Words which is a hands-on activity where the students manipulate a closed set of letters to build words. The words are then sorted so rules about how words work can be created or extended.

It also includes a Word Wall. This permanent bulletin board displays words the children need to read and write. Five words are added to the wall each week. The first day the words are added, the children concentrate on how to write these words with correct handwriting. The next four days the children may write any five words on the wall. The teacher may give clues to make it more fun, e.g., the next word begins with *t* and rhymes with *hen*. After the five words are written, the children turn the paper over and write another word, for example, *in*. The teacher then shows them how to add letters to make a word they know, *in* to make *pin, pins, skin, win*, and *wins*. They also learn how to use the words to form to other words.

Finally, cross-checking teaches the children how to use context and letter knowledge to problem-solve unknown words. There are also other activities that help children use rhyming words and words they know to figure out new words that use the same spelling patterns. A more detailed description of these activities and more can be found in *Phonics They Use: Words for Reading and Writing* (Cunningham, 1995).

Setting It Up

Word Work is one of the easiest activities to add to your schedule. To make a word wall, you need to find a place in the classroom for a permanent bulletin board. Put the alphabet up. Leave spaces between the letters. There will be word cards underneath each letter, and if the letters are too close together the words will overlap. Also leave at least 18" (46 cm) between rows. Caution: you will be surprised at how many of the words start with *t* and *w*, so leave extra room around these letters. The word wall can also be set up under the alphabet that is above the board. It may be necessary to separate the letters to make more room for the words. Add the words below the letters. Once the letters are up, you are ready to go.

Print the words on colored construction paper. The color and shape of the word will help some students remember it. Remember, add about five new words a week. Make a big production when the words are introduced. Have the children clap them out and model proper handwriting.

```
aA        bB          cC          dD

at        be

as

away


eE        fF          gG          hH

each
```

To pick words for the wall, analyze student writing. If there are common words that are being misspelled, add them to the wall. At the beginning of first grade, the first words that go up include *like, went, my, to,* and *can* because these are words that children need in their writing. For a list of 100 common high-frequency sight words, refer to page 6.

If there are common words that are being misspelled, add them to the wall.

In addition to the high-frequency words, put up words that will help children remember the common rimes. A rime is a pattern of letters that begins with a vowel. As Wylie and Durrell (1970) point out, nearly 500 primary grade words can be derived from a set of only 37 rimes. Words that contain these rimes allow the teacher to point out useful strategies for identifying unknown words and spelling. For example, if *name* is a word on the word wall, ask children to write *name* and then write *tame*. Students learn to take off the onset (the beginning consonant or consonant group) and add the onset *t* needed for *tame*. Likewise, give children words to identify, such as *same*, and have the children find on the word wall the word that will help them figure it out.

The 37 rimes follow:

```
-ack     -ail     -ain     -ake     -ale     -ame     -an
-ank     -ap      -ash     -at      -ate     -aw      -ay
-eat     -ell     -est     -ice     -ick     -ide     -ight
-ill     -in      -ine     -ing     -ink     -ip      -ir
-ock     -oke     -op      -ore     -or      -uck     -ug
-ump     -unk
```

Just using the sight word list, nine of the rimes will already be posted on the board. For the rest, try to pick out a word from the thematic unit or a word that will be easy for students to remember, like *name, whale, tank*. You may even want to add picture clues next to these words.

Sight Words

Flash Cards

To help you teach sight words, create flash card patterns. Write on the flash card patterns the sight words you want to teach and reproduce a set for each child. Enlarge and laminate a classroom set of flash cards. Give each child an envelope with a fastener to keep their flash cards in. Follow this same procedure as you introduce new sight words. Here are 100 recommended high-frequency sight words.

the	what	him	has
and	we	she	way
a	can	an	bike
to	this	or	make
in	not	no	did
you	she	my	because
of	your	which	more
it	when	would	two
is	had	each	day
he	as	how	will
that	know	where	come
was	on	go	get
for	up	about	down
I	out	could	now
his	there	time	little
they	do	look	than
with	from	them	too
are	were	many	first
be	so	see	been
but	her	like	who
at	by	these	people
one	if	me	its
said	their	words	water
all	some	into	long
have	then	use	find

For Making Words, the children need individual letter cards with lowercase on one side and uppercase on the other. Make the vowels a different color (either the background paper or the marker) from the consonants. The teacher needs an enlarged set to use in a pocket chart. The teacher also needs to write the words that the children will make on 4" x 6" (10 cm x 15 cm) cards for sorting. The teacher uses a pocket chart for the letters and words. The children can use a simple tray made from strips of index paper (like a used manila folder). About a half inch (1.3 cm) is folded over and stapled on either end. The rest of the folder can be used to make the letter cards (Cunningham, 1995).

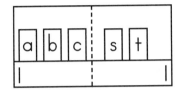

Guided Reading

Guided Reading is similar to a basal approach in that the class works with multiple copies of leveled text. Guided reading takes place after the students have a basic idea about the conventions of print.

The essentials of guided reading are that the teacher explains and/or demonstrates for children the important things to be done while we read. The teacher follows the lead of the students, allowing them to do all the work that they can, and stepping in to support the reader when help is needed. Guided reading is needed when children are reading texts that present new difficulties and require the use of new strategies. In reality, much of what teachers do is to support thinking (Cunningham and Allington, 1999, p. 54).

Writing Workshop

Writing Workshop gives students time to put their thoughts and words into print, thus using the phonics skills and sight words they have been learning. The McCrackens (1995) advocate that this is the best place to teach phonics. As students learn more about letters, sounds, and spelling patterns, they are able to practice by encoding their own ideas.

There is a wealth of material available that explains different ways to set up a writing workshop. One excellent resource is Teacher Created Materials' *Writing Workshop: Lessons and Activities for the Writing Process.* It provides mini-lessons to set up and then maintain a Writing Workshop. The lessons include both skills and the writing process. A sample of one of these mini-lessons can be found on page 9. It also includes forms and materials lists. For a first-person account of one teacher's experiences with Writing Workshop, try *And with a Light Touch* by Carol Avery.

> **Writing Workshop gives students time to put their thoughts and words into print, thus using the phonics skills and sight words they have been learning.**

Independent Reading

Independent Reading gives the children time to select books. By establishing a set routine and coupling the reading with a time—either daily or weekly—to share with classmates, most children can and will enjoy reading for 20 to 30 minutes a day. Helping children select their reading material is critical for the success of this portion of the day. Book baskets where the reading materials have been presorted, either by author, level, or interest, help prevent students from spending their time looking for books instead of reading (Cunningham and Allington, 1999).

By setting up instruction around these four blocks, four approaches to reading are covered. The teacher has provided four different routes to literacy. The guided reading time helps children develop the strategies they need to think while they are reading. This is the key to comprehension.

Children need to see that learning to read and write is something worth doing.

Reading Readiness

For those children who come to school without the motivation to read and write, teachers must include activities that demonstrate that reading and writing are skills the children want and can learn. We assume that children automatically understand the value of reading and writing. This is not the case. Teachers cannot change a child's background or socioeconomic status. What teachers can do is "create literacy-rich environments within our classrooms" (Cunningham and Allington, 1999, p. 22). For the most part, this means providing a variety of realistic reading and writing experiences.

Children need to see that learning to read and write is something worth doing. This means finding topics that interest them or that they want to learn more about. It means finding different types of reading, such as newspapers and reference materials that show the usefulness of reading. Children also need real reasons to write, even if this starts with a wish list or a request for information.

By giving children opportunities to experiment with reading and writing, building their confidence in their own ability to read and write, and showing them how reading and writing are useful to them, teachers help students become motivated learners.

Parts of a Story

Story Parts

Activity:

Students will identify the three primary parts of a story and connect them with the basic story elements.

Materials:

- any favorite storybook
- chart paper
- marking pen

Preparation:

1. Select any favorite story and preread it for the story elements: setting, characters, problem, and solution.
2. Prepare the frame for a large story web on chart paper. A story web lists all the elements of a story.

Directions:

Let the students know that there are three parts to every good story: the beginning, the middle, and the ending. In many stories, the story elements appear in particular parts. The beginning usually contains the setting and the introduction of the characters. Some additional character development may occur, and the problem appears in the middle of the story. The problem is solved and the story concluded in the ending section of the story. Stories written according to this structure are the simplest to write. (Do not be surprised if many stories your students write in the future are three pages in length when published: one page for each part of the story.)

Read to the students the story you have selected. When finished, complete the story web as a class. After completing the web, ask the children in which part of the story each element is introduced. Add this information to your web. Title the chart "Parts of a Story."

Display the chart in the classroom for the children's future reference.

Parts of a Story
• Beginning
—Setting
—Characters Introduced
• Middle
—Characters Developed
—Problem(s)
• Ending
—Solution(s)

Concluding Remarks

Research has shown that readers are subject to the Matthew effect (Stanovich, 1986). Children who are good readers become even better. Children who are not good readers stop reading and fail to improve. This critical fork in the road usually comes in third grade. This deadline puts extreme pressure on early literacy teachers. There is no time to waste on anything that will not help children become good readers.

We always seem to be searching for the single quick fix that will solve the problems of American schools. We mandate, bandwagon, proselytize, alienate, and continue our ever-reforming educational innovations. Perhaps it is time for us to realize that:

1. *There is no quick fix.*

2. *We have actually learned quite a lot about schooling and teaching reading to all children.*

3. *Achieving literacy for all children isn't such a simple matter that it can be blamed on the method of teaching when it does not succeed, even though this is about the only factor we ever debate (Cunningham and Allington, 1994).*

One way to avoid this oversimplification is to implement a balanced reading program. To do this, "the teacher must understand why each activity is included. The teacher must understand the needs to which each activity was intended to respond so that its importance can be assessed with respect to the particular needs of the students. The teacher must understand how the activities fit together in rationale, dependence and independence, and priority" (Adams, 1990, p. 423). In other words, the most important component of a balanced program is you!

> **There is no time to waste on anything that will not help children become good readers.**

Rationale for Guided Reading for Beginning Readers

Constructivism and Learning to Read

In the 1960s Marie Clay began longitudinal studies of children's early literacy progress. Her first study recorded what children were saying and doing in reading and writing from the time they entered school at age five through their sixth birthdays. In addition, mothers kept diaries of the literacy activities the children were producing at home. Further observations were made at ages seven and eight to capture progress in subsequent years.

These observations led to a theory that the child's early reading and writing experiences are used to construct a network of problem solving strategies. This network ties everything a child knows about reading, writing, language, and general (background) knowledge into a system that can be accessed when reading difficulties are encountered. The problem could be an unknown word, not understanding the author's meaning, unusual grammar, etc.

The most critical aspect of this network, is that as it is used, the child generates further learning.

The most critical aspect of this network is that as it is used the child generates further learning (Clay, 1991). In other words, the children are using teacher input and item knowledge such as letter identification, sounds, word families, print conventions, phonemic awareness, and personal experiences to construct the strategies they need to read. Once the child has a system started, every reading event provides feedback needed to extend the system further.

Curriculum

Clay maintains that the best reading approach is one that allows the teacher to assess the child's strengths and help the child apply these strengths to create an effective network of strategies. Item knowledge is useless unless it can be accessed appropriately by the child.

Many reading approaches oversimplify the reading process and lead the teacher to believe that if the child can decode the words, recognize enough sight words, or learn any one aspect of reading in isolation, the child will be a good reader. It is not this simple.

The good reader manipulates language, spatial and visual perception cues, and categorizes these efficiently, searching for dissonant rela-

tions and best-fit solutions. Familiar responses become habitual, require less and less processing and allow attention to reach out towards new information that was not previously noticed. While reading, the reader can construct larger chunks or units of information out of smaller ones, or break large units down into smaller ones for closer examination (Clay, 1991, p. 321).

It appears that some students are able to create this complex problem-solving system on their own. However, poor readers do not. They seem to create a list of the specific things they know how to do. They do not construct a way to use more than one thing on the list at a time. They do not skip from one strategy to another or use story or print information to cross-check their ideas. In other words, they have a ladder, not a net, of responses when they encounter difficulty. Needless to say, it is much more difficult to climb a ladder than fall into a net. In addition, there is not much motivation to keep climbing when everything that has been tried has not worked and there is no reason to believe that the answer will be found by climbing further.

Teacher as Observer

The teacher must be a careful observer of reading behavior. By listening to a child read aloud and analyzing the errors and corrections the child makes, the teacher has a window into what the child is doing in his or her head to solve reading problems. This gives the teacher information to make decisions about what challenges are needed. It also provides information about what strategies the child is using as well as the words that are known (Clay, 1991).

The text the teacher selects is critical. It must not be so easy that the child does not experience any difficulties. On the other hand, 90 to 95 percent of the words should not present any challenge. As the child works, he or she is rewarded when a previously used strategy works. If it does not work, the child must examine why and adjust his or her strategies accordingly. In dealing with either outcome, the child is able to extend his or her net instead of just adding another rung to a ladder.

Observable reading behaviour provides evidence of all the things teachers always thought it did—knowing words, getting meaning, using a sense of story, and working on unknown words in some way. It also includes directional behaviour, recognizing letters or pronounceable clusters, working to get the word sequence right, reading fluently, and locating and correcting error. Such behaviors signal that, inside the child's head, other kinds of activity have possibly occurred like:

- *anticipating what could follow*
- *searching for more 'information' in the print*

It appears that some students are able to create this complex problem-solving system on their own.

- *self-monitoring, evaluating and correcting processes*
- *linking to prior knowledge*
- *lining up a new item with an existing general rule and perhaps extending that rule (Clay, 1991, p. 321).*

Clay sees each child making a singular journey to master reading. Each child's progress varies because his or her starting point is different and what he or she understands and makes sense of is different. Because children are constructing their own networks, any confusions or difficulties must be addressed individually.

This seems to imply that an individual reading approach would be the best. However, this is not practical, even with reduced student numbers, unless the child has access to individual tutoring or is being home schooled.

Guided Reading

In order to be effective in the classroom, the teacher needs a practical way to closely observe the reading behaviors of children. One forum for this is in a small group. The teacher then presents challenges the children can use to develop their personal networks of reading strategies. *Guided reading occurs when:*

- *A teacher works with a small group.*
- *Children in the group are similar in their development of a reading process and are able to read about the same level of text.*
- *A teacher introduces the stories and assists children's reading in ways that help to develop independent reading strategies.*
- *Each child reads the whole text.*
- *The goal is for children to read independently and silently.*
- *The emphasis is on reading increasingly challenging books over time.*

Children are grouped and regrouped in a dynamic process that involves ongoing observation and assessment (Fountas and Pinnell, 1996, p. 4).

Reading Strategies

What are the strategies that are required for a child to construct a network instead of a ladder of item knowledge? There are some strategies that readers need to use on almost all texts. These include the following:

- *calling up relevant background knowledge*
- *predicting what will be learned and what will happen*
- *making mental pictures or 'seeing it in your mind'*

In order to be effective in the classroom, the teacher needs a practical way to closely observe the reading behaviors of children.

13

- *self-monitoring and self-correction*
- *using fix-up strategies such as rereading, pictures, and asking for help when you can't make sense of what you read*
- *determining the most important ideas and events and seeing how they are related*
- *drawing conclusions and inferences based on what is read*
- *deciding 'what you think'—Did you like it? Did you agree? Was it funny? Could it really happen?*
- *comparing and contrasting what you read to what you already know*
- *figuring out unknown words*
- *summarizing what has been read (Cunningham and Allington, 1999, p. 55).*

What is the difference between traditional reading groups and guided reading?

Traditional Reading Groups

Reading groups have been around for a long time. What is the difference between traditional reading groups and guided reading groups? Traditional reading groups tend to emphasize reading accuracy. As soon as a mistake is made, it is corrected by the teacher or another student. This gives the child no time to learn to recognize and fix errors. It also gives children the idea that reading is saying the right word.

Additionally, in round-robin reading each child generally reads just a portion of the text. Ideally, the children follow along as another child reads. If they do not, the whole point of reading is lost. None of the strategies that deal with comprehension and using meaning can be developed. This leaves for the children the task to correctly decode only the words in their sections. No wonder children became word callers instead of readers.

Guided Reading Groups

Guided reading groups are managed differently. First, the teacher selects an appropriate text. The teacher introduces the book in the early days by previewing the story with the pictures. The teacher then may direct the students' attention to different features of the text. He or she may even have the children locate a critical word in the text.

Then, each child whisper-reads the entire text. Eventually, the children read silently. As they are reading, the teacher listens to one child at a time. If a student gets stuck, the teacher prompts the child to use a strategy that might help. After the story is finished, the group talks about the meaning of the text. In addition, the teacher points out good work and successful strategies the students used to solve problems.

At the end of the session, the teacher may take a running record for one student. This is just one method of recording exactly what was read and how. This record is analyzed by the teacher and used to make further text selections and determine which strategies or skills should be taught next.

Homogeneous Grouping

Guided reading is set up using homogeneous groups. This means that the students are all at approximately the same ability level. However research suggests (Juel, 1988) that when children are assigned to the bottom group, they seldom make it out of that group.

Whether this is due to teacher expectations, the child's self-image, different instructional methods, or assigned practice is unclear. In traditional reading groups where the development of strategies was not the goal, the children in the bottom group went slower and spent more time working on word recognition. When children are developing strategies, the grouping is much more dynamic.

Just as learning to talk is a self-extending system—each conversation improves the child's ability to talk—so too must reading be a self-extending system.

Another issue that may be problematic is the work assigned to students not working with the teacher. Traditionally, seatwork did not include much reading or writing. Also, students were not receiving instruction or interacting with their teacher or peers. The chapter on "Organizing a Balanced Program for Beginning Readers" will explore different ways this issue can be addressed.

Concluding Remarks

Reading is a complex behavior, in many ways similar to learning to talk. Just as learning to talk is a self-extending system—each conversation improves the child's ability to talk—so too must reading be a self-extending system.

However, for children learning to talk, adults have mastered appropriate responses to guide them along. It does not just happen naturally. Adults have learned the appropriate responses from their ancestors over the centuries. Adults do not even consciously know what they are doing. It is almost instinctual (Cambourne, 1988).

No such set of instinctual responses exists for teaching children to read. In thinking it through, it makes sense that by observing student behavior, analyzing what may have prompted the behavior, and crafting an appropriate response, the teacher can help students create a self-extending reading system. This process of observation, analysis, and response is key to developing and conducting guided reading lessons. "Planning Guided Reading Lessons for Beginning Readers" will explain how. Read on!

Planning Guided Reading Lessons for Beginning Readers

There are several components to organizing guided reading lessons. The first step is to assess the students. This allows the teacher to determine their strengths. Knowing their strengths allows the teacher to select texts and design the lessons. Ongoing assessment lets the teacher know how effective instruction is.

After students are grouped the teacher plans lessons. Before the lesson, the teacher matches the skills and strategies of the students to a particular book. Usually books are leveled to make this selection easier. Then the teacher plans a book introduction. The words that the children need to recognize are analyzed. Finally, the teacher chooses one or two teaching points that can be demonstrated with the text.

During the lesson, the teacher closely observes student behavior. The assumptions made prior to the lesson may not hold true. The teacher must be flexible in adjusting any or all of the lesson.

After the lesson, the teacher may make a reading record of one or more of the children in addition to making quick notes of other observations. When the next lesson is being planned, the reading record and notes will be analyzed. This analysis will include determining if any of the students have been misplaced in the group. The teacher then selects the book for the next lesson, and the process begins again.

Each of these components of guided reading bears further examination.

Assessment

Assessment usually involves determining students' literacy strengths. Initial assessments as well as ongoing assessments are used for a variety of purposes. Primarily, assessments are to inform instruction. They can also be used to group or regroup students. The assessments give the teacher snapshots of student progress—what item knowledge has been mastered, and what strategies the students are using, and what should be tackled next? They provide feedback about how well instruction is going. They also give detailed information for reporting student progress to parents and administration.

Assessments should be easy to collect and systematic, should provide reliable and valid information, include both formal and informal measures, and should give the teacher the data needed to make the critical decisions required in planning lessons (Fountas and Pinnell, 1996).

The documentation is important because even with reduced class sizes, very few teachers are able to keep and access everything they know about every child. A mother with one or two children can track the progress of her child who is learning to talk. This is what allows her to provide the appropriate feedback. This is impossible for most classroom teachers without a systematic way of collecting, recording, and organizing the information.

What types of assessments are useful? Begin with item knowledge and continue with evaluating how well the child uses the following:

- letter identifications
- letter sounds
- phonemic awareness
- print conventions
- word tests
- writing
- reading records

> **The documentation is important because even with reduced class sizes, very few teachers are able to keep and access everything they know about every child.**

The results of these assessments are summarized and usually kept in a literacy folder maintained by the teacher. The teacher uses this information to plan lessons. Another benefit is that literacy information is passed along when children are promoted or transfer to a new school.

The purpose and scope of each test is listed below.

Letter Identification

This test simply determines if the child recognizes uppercase and lowercase letters by name. All the letters are checked each time the assessment is taken. Do not assume that once a student identifies a letter correctly, it is a permanent condition.

Consider the importance of this information to children. It allows them to attend to the right thing when the teacher says to look at the letter *t* or to have an idea of what to write when a word is spelled out. Caution: many children are able to recognize letters but are unable to write them when given the name or sound.

Letter Sounds

Using lowercase letters, the child says the usual sound associated with each letter. The student receives credit if a word beginning with the sound is given instead of just the sound, for example, mommy instead of /m/. This is because the usefulness of this knowledge is to identify or confirm a word containing the letter. If the child makes the connection that mountain begins the same way as mommy because they both start with the same letter, then the alphabetic principle is being used.

Phonemic Awareness

At some point, children discover that the words they say are made of smaller, identifiable units or sounds. There are various levels of phonemic awareness:

- ability to hear separate words in a sentence
- ability to hear rhymes and then to generate rhymes
- ability to hear syllables in a word
- ability to hear and identify the beginning, ending, and medial sounds in a word
- ability to blend individual sounds and say the word
- ability to segment a word into its individual sounds

A child who cannot blend individual sounds and hear the word is unable to make sense of sounding it out. On the other hand, blending can be and is learned as students learn to read. Segmenting is learned as students ear spell or translate sounds into letters when hearing them.

For an analysis of the research on this topic, refer to Chapter 4 of *Beginning to Read* by Marilyn Jager Adams. For a more practical approach, refer to Teacher Created Materials' *Phonics: Phonemic Awareness Word Recognition Activities.*

Print Conventions

There are conventions about how our language is written. In general, these are arbitrary rules that dictate top to bottom, left to right for words and letters within words, return sweep, spaces between words, and punctuation. These rules seem so obvious to experienced readers that they are often not taught to beginning readers. However, for the student with little reading experience, these underlying assumptions are critical to success.

If a child does not look at the letters in a word in a linear fashion, it is difficult to figure out the usefulness of the alphabetic principle. For example, if the child looks at the word fish and looks at the *h* first, then the *f,* and finally the *i-s* it will be hard to see how these letters can help identify it as the word that has the following sounds in the following order: /f/ /i/ /sh/—fish. Imagine how difficult it is to match words to speech if the words are looked at in the wrong order or only one letter is looked at instead of the set of letters that make up the word.

Many children come to school with these concepts in place due to their

> **A child who cannot blend individual sounds and "hear" the word is unable to make sense of "sounding it out."**

early reading and writing experiences at home or preschool. However, some children do not. These concepts must be taught. This is an important objective of shared reading. It can also be addressed in shared or interactive writing. If there is a group of children who still do not have these concepts, these shared reading and writing lessons may be used as guided reading lessons.

Marie Clay (1993) explains testing procedures in *An Observation Survey of Early Literacy Achievement*. Print conventions can also be evaluated with a checklist as a child is reading, writing, or participating in group lessons. An example of such a checklist follows.

Print Convention Checklist

- ☐ Can identify the front of a book.
- ☐ Can put the title in the right place on a blank book.
- ☐ Can identify where the text is.
- ☐ Can demonstrate how to read text with more than one line (left to right, top to bottom, return sweep).
- ☐ Can match word to word.
- ☐ Can point to the beginning and end of a sentence.
- ☐ Can identify punctuation.
- ☐ Can identify upper and lower case letters.
- ☐ Can identify a single word and a single letter.
- ☐ Can locate the first and last letter in a word and the first and last word in a sentence.

There are many things that can be learned by analyzing childrens' writing.

Writing

There are many things that can be learned by analyzing childrens' writing. How well are they able to discriminate and reproduce the differences among letters? Is their letter formation correct? How many words can they write from memory? Are they able to listen to the words in a sentence and encode them? What spelling patterns have they learned?

If it is not possible to determine this information from several samples of writing, then additional tasks, such as dictation, writing all known words, or a developmental spelling inventory (Gentry, R., 1981; Bear, D. R., Invernizzi, M., Templeton, S., and Johnston, F., 1996) can be used to gain additional information.

Reading Record

There are a variety of ways to record the reading behavior. Many teaching credential programs require a preservice course that provides experience with reading inventories. The important thing is to record information quickly while the child is reading. When the teacher reviews the record later, it should accurately reflect the student's reading behavior.

Marie Clay's *An Observation Survey of Early Literacy Achievement* (1993) provides a detailed description of taking a running reading record. In addition, this book contains practical procedures for five other measures, including letter identification, word test, print conventions, written word inventory, and dictation. Directions for administrating the assessments, including forms and how to score them, are included.

It is important to realize that reporting to the district or parents is just one use of assessments. Teachers are the ones who are held accountable for the progress of their students. By learning how to take and use these assessments, the teacher has invaluable, valid, and reliable information to use in lesson planning (Fountas and Pinnell, 1996).

Grouping

The most efficient way to make an initial grouping of the students is to create a table that contains the children's names and the assessment information that is available. Choose one assessment, such as the reading record, and list the children in order according to this score. If an electronic spreadsheet or database is used, such as in *ClarisWorks* or *Microsoft Excel*, the process becomes even easier as the records can be sorted for any of the assessments.

In the example below, the teacher had a letter identification (LID) score, some word test (WT) scores, and phonemic awareness (PA) scores. The children were originally listed according to their phonemic awareness scores. Later, reading records (RR) were added. The reading levels of the texts were based on the Reading Recovery levels. Please note that this is a multi-age classroom for children in grades one and two. These were the incoming first grade students.

	A	B	C	D	E	F
1	LID	WT	PA	RR	Comments	Name
2						
3	52		New	0		Lydia
4	52		New	3		Peter
5	48	1	8	0		Josh
6	52	1	9	0		Matt
7	21	2	14	0		Ed
8	52	5	42	3		Sarah
9	52		42	1		Ken
10	52		45	3		Ann
11	52		46	0	No word boundaries	Misty
12	52	5	47	1		Chuckie
13						

Initially the students were grouped into two groups (four for the entire classroom) as follows: Group 1: Lydia, Josh, Matt, Ed, and Misty; Group 2: Peter, Sarah, Ken, Ann, and Chuckie. Although Misty had good item knowledge, further analysis revealed that she was unable to use this information strategically during reading. In addition, even with several individual reminders during writing, she did not put spaces between words. So, initially she will be put in the group where these print conventions will be taught.

In guided reading groups, because the emphasis is on the strategies that the children employ as opposed to general ability, the groupings will change during the year. As the teacher has more information about a student, he or she may be regrouped to better meet his or her needs.

Book Leveling

It makes sense that books present different levels of difficulty. A child who has just mastered *The Chick and the Duckling* is not going to be able to read *The Indian in the Cupboard*. Look around at the materials in schools. Reading series have levels within grade levels. Supplementary materials contain reading levels—some by grade level, some in a general sequence. There are Reading Recovery numbered levels. There are formulas to determine readability. There are interest levels. *Guided Reading* (Fountas and Pinnell, 1996) presents alphabetic levels. Even libraries separate easy readers from chapter books and children's books from adult books.

> **Leveling is not anything more than common sense and analyzing the experiences of the students reading the texts.**

All these different systems make leveling seem confusing. Leveling is not anything more than common sense and analyzing the experience of the students reading the text. Before looking at leveling, it is useful to look at the skills beginning readers bring to the task.

Profile of a Beginning Reader

Beginning readers have limited visual perception skills. Some can do the following while others cannot: discriminate one letter from another, connect a sound to a particular letter, recognize that spaces between letters indicate word boundaries, slow their speech down to say something word by word, or recognize a familiar letter pattern such as "at" or "ing."

What all children do have is a basic understanding of how the world works. Again, this may or may not be very sophisticated depending on how much and what types of life experiences they have had. But, on a basic level, children know that if you step in water, your foot gets wet. They also know how to talk. Again, depending on the support prior to school, including the home language, this ranges from language that is limited to simple sentences that facilitate survival to the language of books and poems.

Even though children come to school with different levels of world and language experiences, children already know how to use this information to function in the world. They are not used to using visual information from a text. To make sure children think while they are reading, they need to be required to read for meaning. In the beginning, their general knowledge (does it make sense?) and language knowledge (does it sound right?) are the most useful ways for children to monitor how successful they are.

As children learn more about the visual characteristics of print, this becomes the most important control. Topic knowledge and language patterns are no longer as important because reading expands the readers' experiences with everything about the world that has been written down. This is what allows readers to learn about things outside their personal experiences and to comprehend dialects and book language.

The visual characteristics of print are what guided reading is all about; moving children from using context and language structure to monitor their success to a reliance on visual information is the ultimate goal of reading.

A Continuum of Leveled Books

It makes sense then that books should be presented in a continuum. Early books will present topics that children are familiar with so they can use their general information. They will present the meaning with words and pictures so the child can check what is read against the meanings the pictures convey. The books will have simple language patterns so children can hear whether they sound right or not.

In the beginning, the teacher's goal is for the child to stop and self-correct when it does not make sense or sound right. The teacher is gradually going to show the child how to check the visual information in the text to ask a further question (does it look right?). This is when the child begins to understand that the goal is to get the exact message from the author, not just a rough idea.

As children have more and more visual information such as familiar letter patterns, sight words, spelling patterns, prefixes, and suffixes at their disposal, they no longer need simple sentences, pictures that also carry the meaning, or familiar topics. They are able to take on more difficult, unfamiliar texts.

Basically, a teacher analyzes the strengths of the children. How far along the continuum from context and structure to using visual information are they? The teacher then analyzes the books available for guided reading and selects one that seems to be a good match for the group. The children read the book. The teacher now uses the results of that reading to determine how good the fit was. Was it too easy?

> The visual characteristics of print are what guided reading is all about; moving children from using context and language structure to monitor their success to a reliance on visual information is the ultimate goal of reading.

Was it harder than it appeared? Did the children enjoy reading it?

It is not practical for busy teachers to analyze their books everyday to prepare for the following day's lessons. This is why books are leveled by publishers. However, publishers are not in your classroom, so the characteristics they feel are important may not work out. This is why Reading Recovery provides its teachers with lists of books with levels that previous teachers have found useful when working with students.

Reading Recovery is a program where one teacher works with one child for about 30 minutes a day. Children are selected because they are making slow progress. Sometimes, what they know about reading is very limited. The idea is that the teacher can accelerate learning by starting with the student's strengths, and he or she will be able to catch up with the class, not just move ahead at a slower rate. Reading Recovery teachers found that dividing books into many very narrow levels was useful.

It is not practical for busy teachers to analyze their books every day to prepare for the following day's lessons.

The guided reading teacher is not working with the same constraints as the Reading Recovery teacher. The children are receiving good instruction and are making progress. The children are not all exactly alike, so the range of books that may be suitable for the group is much broader. *Guided Reading: Good First Teaching for All Children* (Fountas and Pinnell, 1996) is an excellent resource that lists the characteristics of different levels and the characteristics of the readers at each level, as well as hundreds of leveled titles from a variety of sources.

In the Lake Elsinore Unified School District in California, another book leveling reference was developed by Elle Robinson, a Reading Recovery teacher/leader, for use in the Balanced Literacy Training course. This chart presents characteristics of books with several Reading Recovery levels grouped together.

Balanced Literacy Training
Texts and Reading Behaviors

Level	Supports	So the child can	Cautions!
1–3 *Early Phonemic Spelling*	• Single idea or simple story line that children can easily relate to • Label books, caption books, patterned, predictable books (usually 1–2 sentences) • High-frequency words used throughout • Direct picture/text match • Clear, consistent text format, starting with one line of text on one page and moving to 2–5 lines on both pages	• control the reading process by knowing what he or she knows and being held responsible to use it! • gain control over directionality and 1:1 voice-to-print match. • use the strongly supported M & S to predict what the text will say and confirm if he or she is reading correctly. • use familiar words as footholds through print and learn new words. • read unknown words using letter cues (mostly first letters, then first and last, then first and a bit more) and checking with meaning. • pay close attention to print, noticing new features of letters and words with each reading. • monitor his or her reading by 1:1 voice/print match, known words, letter cues, and mismatches between meaning and structure.	• Some books take the child out of control by having first or last pages that the child cannot read at this point. The teacher must tell the child what these pages say, and the child might think reading is memorizing what the teacher tells him or her and remembering the pattern. • Label and caption books have limited relation to how we talk—there is often not enough language structure to support readers. • Some books contain concepts and vocabulary that are unfamiliar to children, especially English-language learners, and have little or no literary value. • Some trade books have poor layouts, fonts, etc., for these beginning readers.
4–6 *Phonemic Spelling*	• Stories are more complex but still very easy to understand. • There are more variations in language patterns, less repetition, and/or patterns may vary. • Pictures are supportive but may show a scene—more attention to print is required. • Print is clear—may be several lines of print per page. • There are variations in word structure (*ing, ed, s,* some contractions, etc).	• control reading of longer texts. • solve some unfamiliar words, using sounding out (basic, cvc, cumulative analysis), analogies to known words (can-fan), and chunks of words (prefixes and suffixes, words in words, consonant blends, and digraphs, etc.). • continue to monitor reading, searching for more information (M, S, V) to make another attempt.	• Children should always be reading for meaning! Sound analysis must be used in conjunction with M & S! • There should be almost no finger pointing. Children must scan print with their eyes. • Children must read with phrasing and expression at a good pace. • Don't rush through this foundational stage.

Elle Robinson, Lake Elsinore Unified School District,© 1997   1

Level	Supports	So the child can	Cautions!
7–9	• Stories are more complex with subtle ideas that will require more interpretation, and there may be more than one episode. • There is greater variety in the way dialogue is presented. • Punctuation is more complex and plays a growing role in phrasing and expression. • Literary language may be mixed with natural language. • Frequently used words continue to expand. • Text placement, format, and print size may vary. • Illustrations may contain several ideas—text carries more of the story line. • Words build on and extend children's vocabulary and frequently used words.	• check one source against another but more attempts should fit M, S, & V in an integrated manner. The child is searching more visual information to come up with a possible pronunciation for a new word and then correcting and/or confirming his or her pronunciation using M & S. • learn more about sound/letter patterns such as the silent <u>e</u> marker and some vowel digraphs. • start to notice and use spelling patterns (<u>fight</u>, s<u>now</u>). He or she asks, "Does this word look right?" Repetitions get shorter perhaps only a few words or a phrase.	• Children must maintain fluent reading. • Writing development and word work must keep pace and support the increased need to visually analyze words at this level. • Book introductions do not necessarily get shorter. These readers may need <u>more</u> support because of the visual work required. • Make sure children are reading many different genres and authors.
10–12	• More challenging ideas, vocabulary and use of literary language • Stories are longer and may contain several episodes. • There is a greater range of content. • Characters are more complex. *Transitional Spelling*	• move through text using print and pictures in an integrated way while attending to meaning. • continue to decipher new words by using word analysis and then confirming words with meanings. • monitor reading over long stretches of text. • self-correct close to point of error, sometimes almost before the error is spoken. • connect text to others. • discuss the text with increasing sophistication. • manage a variety of texts—fiction and informational texts.	• As students read more difficult texts, remember that it is still important for them to read and reread many easy, familiar texts at school and home for fluency, comprehension, and orchestration of reading strategies. • Make sure the <u>child</u> is doing the problem solving, not you!
13–16	• Variety of texts—including informational • Written language structure • Specialized vocabulary for some topics that may be unusual or challenging • Illustrations provide low-moderate support.	• decipher new words competently on initial reading. • demonstrate less over problem-solving and moves through text more fluidly. • **begin reading to learn!**	• Provide support for reading different genres: format, vocabulary, purpose, and concepts. • Give students lots of time to read and reread easy, familiar text. • Discussion/responding to texts is vital.

Elle Robinson, Lake Elsinore Unified School District,© 1997

2

25

All lists are subject to change. Teachers make mistakes. If a book is presented and it is a bad fit, make a note. Assumptions made about the group may be incorrect, but it is also possible that the book is leveled incorrectly. Both the Fountas and Pinnell and the Reading Recovery lists have ways to provide feedback to the list keepers.

Planning Lessons

The assessments are completed, the children have been tentatively grouped, an approximate book level has been determined, and now it is time to prepare the lesson.

First, the teacher selects a text. The text should appeal to the children. When looking through the books at approximately the right level, these factors should also be considered.

The text should appeal to the children.

- *Are the concepts in the book familiar to children, or can they be made accessible through the introduction?*
- *Is the plot interesting? Will it appeal to this group of children?*
- *Does the text provide opportunities for this group of children to use what they know?*
- *Are some words in the book known to children?*
- *Are other words accessible through children's current ability to use strategies such as word analysis and prediction from language structure or meaning?*
- *Do the illustrations support children's search for meaning? Do they extend the meaning of the text?*
- *Is the length of text appropriate for the experience and stamina of the group?*
- *For emergent and early readers, is the the layout clear? Is the print clear? Are there an appropriate number of lines of text? Is there sufficient space between words? (Fountas and Pinnell, 1996, p. 135)*

Book Introductions

Once the text is selected, the teacher needs to prepare an introduction. The introduction accomplishes several purposes. First, it addresses the fact that the students in the group are not all alike. This means that no matter how carefully the text has been selected, the text will provide different levels of support for different students. Second, the introduction models what good readers do before reading. Good readers have an idea about what the book is going to be like before they begin reading. They may have read the back cover, a book by the same author, or read a review; they may be familiar with the genre or have background knowledge about the subject. Third, the introduction provides any further support the students may need to successfully negotiate the text.

The introduction should also be interactive. The teacher leads a discussion about what the children should expect. The discussion can range from a great deal of support to just a couple of ideas to get the children started. The long-term goal is for a student to pick up a book and read it without an introduction. Fountas and Pinnell (1996, p. 137) list several things that can be included in an introduction.

- *Draw on the children's experience and knowledge.*
- *Leave room for the children to bring their experiences to bear on the story.*
- *Explain important ideas and concepts.*
- *Discuss the plot or theme of the whole story.*
- *Say (and sometimes have children repeat) language patterns that are unfamiliar and are critical to the story.*
- *Talk about the meaning of the whole story.*
- *Talk about the illustrations and help children discover information in them.*
- *Discuss the characters in the story.*
- *Draw children's attention to the structure of the text and help them understand "how the book works."*
- *Occasionally address letter-sound relationships or clusters in the pronunciation of unfamiliar words (proper names, for example).*
- *Use some of the new and challenging vocabulary found in the story.*
- *Draw children's attention to specific words and punctuation.*
- *Explore any aspects of text layout that affect the meaning of the story or would be tricky for children to follow.*

A follow-up to this would be to "Leave the children with one or two clear questions that will drive them into the text and serve as a continuing impulse to seek meaning when they read" (Holdaway, 1979, p. 143).

The long-term goal is for a student to pick up a book and read it without an introduction.

The best way to learn how to do an introduction is by plotting it out, presenting it, and then monitoring how effective it was by how prepared the students were. The introduction is not meant to ensure perfect reading. It is meant to provide enough support so the readers can use and develop their own reading strategies.

One way to prepare for guided reading lessons is to keep notes in a second plan book. This keeps track of the books read, and sticky notes can be attached to record comments during the lesson. The plans for two guided reading lessons follow. The first lesson is for children who are reading independently (95% accurately) Reading Recovery level three texts. They understand print conventions and know several sight words. The second lesson is for a group of children who are reading independently at Reading Recovery levels 16 to 24. The introduction does not focus on reading difficulties as much as the background needed to understand the text.

Monday	
Group: Karen's Book: *Animals Hide* Pattern: A _ is hiding in a/the _. Anchor words: *a, the, is, in, see* Intro: <u>Look</u> at this picture. <u>Who</u> is hiding? Why is it hard to <u>see</u>? Picture walk: <u>Who</u> is hiding? Where is it hiding? This is coral. Do you know how coral grows? In a reef. Use see —> reef. Use first letter—> cave. Can you see that the fawn is in the shade? Look at this word— reeds. What word (see) would help us? Yes, the duck is hiding in the reeds. Show me where the reeds are in the picture. Now, can you point to the word reeds. Where is the snake? Can you find the word that tells you? On the last page, one of the words is *who*. What do you think the ending letter of who is. Can you find this word?	Group: JR's Book: *Pompeii... Buried Alive* Intro: Look at the picture on the cover. What does it tell you about the story? Let's read the back cover to find out a little more about this book. Talk about and say Pompeii, Mount Vesuvius—point out that "yes" and "us" will help them pronounce and remember Vesuvius. Show where Pompeii is on map/globe. What was life like 2,000 years ago? Look through the pictures in the first chapter and talk about them. I'm sure you're anxious to find out what happens. Let's read the first chapter and then we'll stop and talk about what we find out.

Teaching for Strategies

During the reading the teacher needs to respond to appeals for help or mistakes so the students build upon the strategies they already have. "...teachers use questions or prompts to help children learn how to think about different sources of information as they put together a flexible system of strategies they can apply on increasingly difficult text. The teacher listens carefully, observes the precise reading behavior, and when appropriate, makes a facilitating response" (Fountas and Pinnell, 1996, p. 160).

There are three broad categories of strategies. First, there are strategies that help maintain fluency. Fluency is important because working at the phrase or sentence level helps the child maintain meaning. Next, there are strategies that help children detect or correct errors. Again, the child first needs to realize something is wrong and then figure out where the mistake is and how to fix it. There also are strategies that help children solve the problems that a new word presents.

The teacher responds with questions that prompt the child to think or use what is already known to solve the problem. A list of possible prompts from Fountas and Pinnell (1996) follows.

To support the control of early reading behaviors:

Read it with your finger.

Did you have enough (or too many) words?

Did it match?

Were there enough words?

Did you run out of words?

Try ____. Would that make sense?

Try ____. Would that sound right?

Do you think it looks like ____?

Can you find ___? (known or new word)

Read that again and start the word.

> There also are strategies that help children solve the problems that a new word presents.

To support the reader's use of self-monitoring or checking behavior:

Were you right?

Where's the tricky word? (after an error)

What did you notice? (after hesitation or stop)

What's wrong?

Why did you stop?

What letter would you expect to see at the beginning? at the end?

Would ____ fit there?

Would ____ make sense?

Do you think it looks like ____?

Could it be ___?

It could be ___, but look at ___.

Check it. Does it look right and sound right to you?

You almost got that. See if you can find what is wrong.

Try that again.

To support the reader's use of all sources of information:

Check the picture.

Does that make sense?

Does that look right?

Does that sound right?

You said (....). Can we say it that way?

You said (....). Does that make sense?

What's wrong with this? (Repeat what the child said.)

Try that again and think about what would make sense.

Try that again and think about what would sound right.

Do you know a word like that?

Do you know a word that starts with those letters?

What could you try?

Do you know a word that ends with those letters?

What do you know that might help?

What can you do to help yourself?

To support the reader's self-correction behavior:

Something wasn't quite right.

Try that again.

I like the way you worked that out.

You made a mistake. Can you find it?

You're nearly right. Try that again.

To support phrased, fluent reading:

Can you read this quickly?

Put your words together so it sounds like talking.

(Fountas and Pinnell, 1996, p. 161)

It may be useful to make charts or cards that list these prompts by category to make them more accessible during the lesson.

> **The teacher may also want to point out a problem that one or two readers had and talk about the strategies used to solve this type of problem.**

After the Lesson

Once the children have finished reading, the teacher should provide some closure. This may involve discussing the story or talking about an interesting part of the story. It may also mean discussing any difficulties the students had. A student may even want to share how a particular problem was solved. The teacher may also want to point out a problem that one or two readers had and talk about the strategies used to solve this type of problem.

Materials and Space Requirements

To conduct a guided reading lesson, in addition to multiple copies of leveled books, the teacher needs the following:

- notepaper
- paper cut into strips (these are used to isolate a word or to write sentences that can be cut apart and resequenced) or 3" x 5" (8 cm x 15 cm) cards
- a white board or chalkboard

- markers or pencils
- paper, white boards, or chalkboards for students to practice high-frequency words or to explore word families (optional)

The teacher also needs a space to conduct the lesson. Many teachers find that a horseshoe table is the best for this type of small group instruction. Other teachers meet on the floor.

One thing that most teachers find challenging is having everyone read at the same time. If the students all start together, some will listen to a neighbor instead of doing their own reading work. Others are so distracted by the oral reading that they are unable to do any reading work. One solution is to have the children set their chairs up in a semicircle. This can be as widely spaced as practical. The teacher sits in a rolling chair. The teacher staggers the start times and stresses that the children are to use their quietest whisper-voices. The teacher can then move from one student to another to listen in on the reading. A signal can also be established so children can let the teacher know they are stuck.

One thing that most teachers find challenging is having everyone read at the same time.

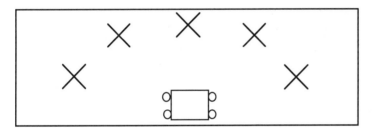

Concluding Remarks

Learning how to read is a very complex process. It makes sense that teaching children to read is also complex. There are things to do prior to teaching, including assessment and leveling books. There are things to do prior to each lesson, selecting the text and preparing the introduction. There are things to do while children are reading, deciding on appropriate prompts and choosing teaching points. There are things to do after the lesson, analyzing the success of the choice of text and the introduction, determining if the grouping is still viable, and determining how to use these observations for future planning.

Just as children need to construct a self-extending system for reading, teachers need to construct a self-extending system for teaching reading. By developing a system for organizing observations and establishing a routine for analyzing these observations, the teacher will begin to create this self-extending system. The good news is that once the system is started, every lesson taught extends the system.

Organizing a Balanced Program for Beginning Readers

Organizing Curriculum

Thematic teaching is one way to extend literacy learning time. It allows you to cover social studies or science topics throughout the day. The biggest advantage is that children come to school with a natural curiosity about the world around them and how things work. By choosing themes that appeal to you and your students, part of the task of motivating the students to learn is already done.

In choosing themes, consider the various sources of "what to teach," the curriculum guides, textbooks, and school requirements. Brainstorm various topics that would include these requirements. In primary grades, the reading series may or may not present stories in a continuum. If it does, then it may be best left to the guided reading portion of the day and not considered in developing themes.

It is important to remember that not every activity or story must relate to the theme. For example, many children's songs and stories lend themselves to innovation. By using a known song pattern and melody, new lyrics can be written that relate to the theme. Using "Three Blind Mice," a song about fish was developed. In this case, teaching the children "Three Blind Mice" was a useful tool to summarize what children had learned about fish. In upper grades, instead of class projects, innovations can be assigned individually or as small group projects.

> Three little fish
> Three little fish
> Swim in schools
> Swim in schools
> They swim in the ocean, the lake, or a brook,
> They have gills and fins to swim, just look,
> They want to swim freely, not swallow a hook,
> Three little fish
> Three little fish.

Another advantage to organizing by theme is the wealth of resource material available. Teacher Created Materials has published over 100 teacher support books for specific themes. Activities from a thematic resource book, TCM 266, *Apples,* are on pages 33 and 34.

Name: | Date:

Parts of an Apple Flower

Work with a partner. Label the parts of this apple flower. Use words from the Word Bank below.

_ _ _ _ _ r

_ t _ _ _ _ _

_ i _ _ _ _ _ _

_ _ _ _ a _ _

_ _ y _ _ _

s _ _ _ _ _

_ _ _ _ _ e

_ _ _ _ _ y

Word Bank

filament	stigma	style	ovule
anther	ovary	sepal	petal

Teacher: You may wish to enlarge this for a wall chart to which students can refer if the activity is too difficult for your group.

33

Name:	Date:

From Tree to Market

Color and cut apart the pictures. Paste them in order in the frame below.

1.	2.	3.	4.

Tell a story. Write a sentence about each picture in order.

1. _____

_____

2. _____

_____

3. _____

_____

4. _____

_____

34

It is also possible to organize using ideas from your teacher's edition. Most teachers' editions include integrated activities as well as skill-based activities that can be used as center ideas.

How to Organize for Guided Reading

How to plan a guided reading lesson has already been discussed. Just as important is what the children not in the current guided reading group are doing. If they are disruptive, if they interrupt the teacher, or if they are not working at worthwhile activities, then the cost of guided reading may exceed its benefits. There are several ways to provide literacy activities during guided reading.

Independent Activities

The children can be assigned one or more different activities that they work on every day while the teacher is working with small groups. There are some disadvantages. There may not be sufficient materials for the entire class. Unless the activity is of a type the children have done successfully before, the chances that the children will be able to do it independently without interrupting the small group is small. Sometimes, in order to make the assignment independent, it is too easy and does not provide appropriate practice for the students. Another consideration is providing for different abilities. In a regular classroom there are a variety of abilities. In a multi-age classroom, these differences are even greater. One assignment may not be appropriate for all students. Several assignments will take more organization (to direct which children do which assignment) and more time to explain.

Just as important is what the children not in the current guided reading group are doing.

Depending on your style and the students, independent activities may work well. A list of possible activities can be made and added to as the children are able to do more. This list could include such things as Read the Room, Read at the Overhead Projector, Work on the Book Project, Work on the Poem Project, Read from your Book Basket, etc.

Alternately, each reading group can be assigned a follow-up activity that lasts about an hour and that the children do after their reading group. A list of what to do if finished early would be available. This would provide for the different levels of difficulty. Parent volunteers or instructional aides may be available to run interference or actually work with small groups of students while you are with the guided reading group. Keep in mind that if each group has its own set of activities, they will tend to work together. This means the children will be homogeneously, not heterogeneously, grouped.

Independent activities provide one way to teach students how to use centers. This usually takes several weeks. During guided reading time, carefully explain the assignment, including the symbolic directions. The first day, plan to be available to assist the students. The next day, plan a similar activity. If the children understand what to do, you may pull individual students for assessment or a small group for instruction. This also provides a way to teach students what your expectations are during guided reading and gives them a chance to practice being independent.

Another option is to devote this time to reading. Children learn to read by reading. They need to read many easy books to develop the automatic word recognition of good readers. You may choose to organize this time as teacher-directed reading where the children read books that you select. These could be books that were previously read in guided reading or books at a level where at least 95 percent of the words are known.

Teach the children a routine for what to do when they get stuck.

The easiest way to organize the works is in book baskets. Establish a basket for each guided reading group. When the children finish reading a book in guided reading, add it to the basket. In addition, books at lower levels can be added to the basket. It is preferable if there are at least two copies of each text as this allows partner reading. However, unlike guided reading, there does not need to be a book for each member of the group.

Partner and Individual Reading

The teacher can assign children to read with a partner or individually (Cunningham and Allington, 1999). Use your experience in determining who is responsible enough to read individually. If possible, pair a struggling reader with a better reader. In a multi-age classroom, pair better older readers with better younger readers and struggling older readers with struggling younger readers. This boosts the confidence of the struggling older readers as the material for the younger readers is usually easy reading for the older readers.

Teach the children a routine for what to do when they get stuck. Prepare a chart that reminds students of what they should try when they get stuck (Cunningham and Allington, 1999). If they are still stuck and their partners cannot help, then the procedure may be going to the aide, to a designated child, or marking the word with a sticky note.

It is important to teach children how to be good partners. If a partner immediately says the word when there is a pause or mistake, this prevents the use of problem-solving strategies by the reader. It is also a good idea to vary the type of partner reading that is expected (Cunningham and Allington, 1999).

The advantage of partner reading is accountability. However, some children will find partner reading stifling, especially if they are motivated readers and are reading silently. For these children, you may want to assign them individual reading from time to time. (They should also participate in partner reading at times as a service to the rest of the class.) This is not independent reading because the child is not choosing what to read. The assigned text could include finishing a reading selection that was introduced in the previous guided reading lesson. The next guided reading lesson will then focus on exploring some aspect of the literature such as story structure, characters, setting, theme, plot, developing a story map, etc.

Directed Writing

Another option is directed writing and handwriting practice. It is critical that children are taught how to do this prior to using it as an independent activity.

To write independently, a child needs four things:

1. ideas, usually developed thematically

2. words, developed in various types of word banks

3. the ability to spell

4. knowledge of the writing structure of the English language (McCracken and McCracken, 1995, p. 133).

There are a variety of writing structures that include lists (the easiest), frame sentences, different types of stories (circular, cumulative, patterned, folk tales, etc.), and poetry. Once the children learn a particular structure, they can then use word banks developed during science or social studies to extend their learning and practice a particular structure of the English language. For example, *Where Do You Live?* uses the pattern: "Do you live in a pig pen? No! No! No! Pigs live in a pig pen." Assume the children are studying Native Americans. They have been working on a unit about homes and lodges. An example of a unit containing such information can be found on page 38.

For independent writing the children use the pattern in *Where Do You Live?* to show what they have learned about traditional Native American dwellings. They might write: "Did you live in a plank house? No! No! No! Haida lived in a plank house. Did you live in a hogan? No! No! No! Navaho lived in a hogan." This lends itself to different abilities. Less able children write less. The writing can also be set up in a booklet format that would require an illustration of each dwelling.

> Once the children learn a particular structure, they can then use word banks developed during science or social studies to extend their learning and practice a particular structure of the English language.

Homes and Lodges

The Earliest Homes

The North American continent spans an area of over 7,000 square miles (11,000 square kilometers). Immigrants from Europe and Asia immigrated to this enormous continent over the centuries, and the population grew until, by the time of Christopher Columbus, there were millions of people living across the land from Alaska to South America.

The earliest Americans, ancestors of contemporary Native Americans, lived in the cold and harsh climate of the Ice Age. Hunters depended upon the large animals grazing along the edge of the ice flows for the meat and fur they could provide. To make a shelter from the cold winds and snow, the furs of animals were fastened to poles of wood or bones. The earliest Americans had the knowledge of fire and made fires in their dwellings and temporary shelters. As the climate became warmer over time, the people began to change their lifestyles to adapt to the new conditions. They also adapted to their particular environment so that homes in one area were possibly quite different from homes in another area.

Adapting to the Environment

The human species is very adaptable to a wide range of habitat and climatic conditions. Humans have survived the hottest deserts and the coldest tundra. They have made permanent and temporary dwellings from wood, bark, animal skins, grass, thatch, mud, and stone, each providing the shelter they needed. Homes were always made from the materials available in each area. In the coldest Arctic, the people built their homes from animal furs, wood, or blocks of ice. In forested areas, homes and lodges were made from planks of wood. Homes were permanent or temporary, depending upon the lifestyle and the season.

Homes Today

Most of the homes in North America today are permanent dwellings, and they are usually quite different from the homes of the past. Even mobile homes are usually parked for years at a time, and some camper vehicles are used as homes. Today, as in the past, there can be a sharp contrast in the housing styles across America. From the city highrise apartments to the isolated homes of the countryside, Americans live alone, with family groups, or with friends, just as they always have. In any of these modern homes, you might find a Native American.

Make sure the students know that the people today usually live in houses that are just like everyone else's. However, to better understand the Native American homes of yesterday, they may enjoy hearing about the different styles of homes made centuries ago. They can make some traditional Native American homes with paper and clay, discuss their present-day homes, and then design homes for the future.

The children can also use this time to practice handwriting. For both directed writing and handwriting, it is important that the children do their best work. To accomplish this requires a combination of high expectations and judicious nagging. This can be done by an instructional assistant, a parent volunteer, or the teacher between guided reading groups.

An advantage of directed writing is that it is easy to extend thematic studies during language arts time. With proper planning, brainstorming, word banks, and initial teaching have already been completed. The patterns help students incorporate literary English structures into their independent writing. In addition, the children are practicing what they have learned (content, writing, and handwriting), a critical step in mastering any skill.

Literacy Learning Centers

A final option is to establish literacy learning centers. Explaining learning centers is a huge undertaking. There are professional books such as Teacher Created Materials' *Learning Centers* and books about how to set up and manage learning centers, such as Teacher Created Materials' *How to Manage Learning Centers in the Classroom*. Learning centers that focus on literacy are described in *Guided Reading* (Fountas and Pinnell, 1996). This section is designed to provide just enough basic information to get you started.

Learning centers allow teachers to meet the needs of all the children in the classroom. Because learning centers are flexible, they offer activities that appeal to different learning styles and ability levels. This in turn minimizes disruption.

There are two major decisions the teacher needs to make to begin. First, decide what centers will be established. Second, decide how will the children be grouped and moved through the centers.

Selecting Centers

Centers should be established that provide meaningful practice. Centers are not designed to teach new skills. The centers should be fairly low maintenance. If it takes hours to set up the centers every day, week, or month, sooner or later there will come a time when there just is no time to prepare.

Centers should offer a variety of activities. Children today do not get up every morning to help milk the cows. In other words, it is difficult for children to do the same thing day after day without complaint, and complaints usually look like disruptive behavior.

On the other hand, students must already know how to do the work.

> Because learning centers are flexible, they offer activities that appeal to different learning styles and ability levels.

If you want to add a new center activity, remember that students must be taught how to do the activity first. Even if the objective is to follow directions, teach the skill to the class when an adult is available to answer questions. When the class has mastered the skill, then it can be added as a center activity.

Possible Literacy Center Ideas

Book Baskets—Provided a basket of books for each guided reading group. The books can be read in groups or are at the students' independent reading levels.

Letters and Words—On a magnetic board or a pocket chart, use letters to make words. For accountability, you may want children to record or have someone check their work.

Listening Center—Children may just listen or listen and respond in some way to prerecorded stories. This center may also be used for children to record themselves reading a story, either individually or in a small group.

Art Center—This type of center may be used to illustrate class books, respond to a story visually, or extend a story.

Writing Center—This can involve directed writing, card or letter writing, response to a story, or a continuation of Writer's Workshop. Do not assign free writing if children also participate in Writer's Workshop. If a child wants to continue working on a project from Writing Workshop, it should be his or her choice.

Reading Around the Room—Read charts, class stories, and classmates' published stories that are posted around the room.

Independent Reading—This promotes self-selected reading (may include a reading log or response).

Partner Reading—Read to a partner; select books from the appropriate book basket.

Drama—Dramatize (act, reader's theater, or puppetry) a story.

Poem Box—Read several poems that have been introduced to the class during shared reading.

Computer—Reading or writing software or teacher directed activities. A sample activity can be found on pages 42 and 43.

Overhead Projector—Prepared transparencies of poems or stories can be introduced in shared reading. Illustrate transparencies to present to the class.

Games—Implement reading or writing games, commercial or teacher made.

Reading Response—There are a number of ways children can respond to their reading. The responses can be on books read aloud in class, during independent reading, or guided reading. An example of two reading responses can be found on pages 44 and 45.

Literature Circles—These are forums for children to discuss a book that all the participants have read. Usually this requires a sign-up sheet.

Pocket Chart—Pocket charts can be used in a variety of ways. They can be used for children to independently repeat a making words lesson (how many different words can you make from these letters?). It can be used to sequence a story that has been copied onto sentence strips. It can be used to put together a poem or story from individual word cards. It can be used to make new sentences or stories by replacing some of the words.

Story Project—In a thematic classroom, there may be a story that is the focus for the week. The story project extends this story in some way. An example of a generic story project can be found on pages 46 and 47.

Poem Project—In a thematic classroom, there may a poem that is the focus for the week. The children may be asked to do a cloze exercise (fill in the missing words), look for words with particular patterns, sequence the lines or the words within lines, or find and record all the Word Wall words found in the poem.

Construction—This can include building materials where the children have the opportunity to make something, e.g., Lego® vehicle, and then label and/or write about what they made, its special features, what the child likes about it, and what would be added or changed next time. This center could have different materials available on different weeks, such as paper, cardboard, boxes, modeling clay, Tinkertoys, materials to create or recreate settings and/or stories, or any other materials the children can use to construct in three dimensions.

Math—This could include having the children sort and graph the words in a story by word length. It could ask children to count and graph the different letters in a sentence or on a page. It could ask children to tally the number of times each word appears in a sentence, on a page, or in a story.

NUMBER WORDS

Students match number words to graphics.

Grade Level: one

Duration: 15 to 20 minutes

Materials: teacher-created electronic work sheet; drawing software, such as *Kid Pix 2* or *SuperPrint*

Before the Computer:

- Students have had several experiences working with number words. They have matched numbers to words and successfully counted and named graphics according to number words.

- The teacher has created a document on which there are several graphics of varying numbers on one side of the document, such as three shoes or five hats. On the opposite side of the document, there are number words which correspond to the graphics on the other side of the screen.

- This document has been saved on individual disks or has been saved on the hard drive of computers as a stationery file.

- Students know how to use tools to draw lines.

On the Computer:

- Students draw lines to match number words to the appropriate graphics.

- Students add their names to their documents, save, and print one copy of each for teacher evaluation (optional).

Extensions:

- This is an easy activity for students to duplicate for classmates. Students place graphics and number words on a draw document. They save their work with a title such as "My Name's Number Words." As students complete this document, they can save in the same manner—"My Name's Number Words."

- The following assessment can be used to evaluate student-created documents.

NUMBER WORDS *(cont.)*

NUMBER WORDS ASSESSMENT			
	Yes	No	Comment
Number words are spelled correctly.			
Correct number of graphics is used.			
Number words are matched correctly.			

Draw lines from the pictures to the matching number words.

two

eight

three

four

one

seven

five

Name _____ Date_____

THE BARE BONES

_____
Title of Story

somebody_____

wanted _____
_____

but _____
_____

so _____
_____

at last, _____
_____

Name _____ Date _____

HOW DOES IT RATE?

Super

A Review of _____

1. What I liked best about this book was _____
   because _____
   _____

2. Another thing I liked was _____
   because _____
   _____

   Good

3. What I did not like about this book was _____
   because _____
   _____

4. The best character was _____
   because _____
   _____

   OK

5. I think the book would be better if _____
   _____
   _____

   Pretty Good

6. One part I would not change is _____
   _____
   _____

7. The person I think would enjoy this book is _____
   _____

   Forget It

To rate the book, use a crayon to color the scale.

DRAMATIZATION

Dramatizing a story is not only fun for children but it can greatly improve their reading skills.

Stick Puppets

Materials: white tagboard, paper, craft sticks or straws, scissors, tape or glue

To prepare:

1. Ask the children to name the characters and objects that play important parts in their stories.

2. Have them draw and color the characters on white paper. They may create their own designs or use the outlines of the figures (pages 138–142). Some characters may need more than one shape.

3. Help them mount their figures on tagboard and secure them to the ends of craft sticks or straws.

To proceed:

- Children are usually very comfortable projecting their ideas through puppets.

- Initially, the puppets may be used to **teach character traits or actions**. As the teacher makes statements about the characters, children can hold up the correct puppets.

- The class can then be divided into small groups to **prepare assigned scenes** from the story. One child can be the narrator, reading from the book as the others operate their puppets.

The children's creativity will quickly take over.

- They can experiment with the puppets, **retelling the story** in their own words.

- They can be innovative by **adding new situations** to the story.

- They can use their books and practice **recognizing dialogue** as they read the character parts aloud.

- They can even use their puppets in **presenting a TV commercial** for their books.

DRAMATIZATION *(cont.)*

Stick Puppet Theater

The children will enjoy having a "home" for their puppets.
(Make one theater for every 2–4 children.)

Materials: colored poster board (¹/₂ sheet for each theater)

To prepare:

1. Cut a piece of colored poster board in half.

2. Fold the sides back.

3. Cut a "window" in the front panel.

4. Let the children personalize and decorate their own theaters.

Shadow Play

In a shadow play, the children use the silhouettes of their puppets to represent objects and characters from a story. Place a simple silhouette representing a character from the story on an overhead projector or in front of another light source. Project it onto a screen or wall. Have the children guess who it represents. They will easily be motivated to use their puppets or create others to make shadows of their own.

Before they present their play, give the children the opportunity to practice projecting their silhouettes in front of a light source.

Determine Which Centers to Set Up First

The materials required for centers varies. The best advice is to think about the type of literacy activities the children in your class are currently doing. If school has not started, take stock of the materials that are available, can be borrowed, or made. Start with centers that can be used over and over, such as a listening center. The only maintenance is to rotate books and tapes.

Then the centers need to be set up (permanently or in storage containers). Each center should include all the materials required to complete the activity and symbolic directions whenever possible. Use icons or symbols to identify the boxes and matching location. For example, a large icon representing book baskets is posted where the book baskets are stored. This same icon is used to direct children to this center. Use color coding. It helps the children return materials to the correct center box.

Start with centers that can be used over and over, such as a listening center.

Learning Center Rotation

There are three basic ways for children to visit centers. The first is free choice. The teacher establishes how many students may visit a center at one time. A student goes to a center. If there is room, he or she takes a ticket or clothespin and participates in the center activity. If there are no tickets or clothespins, the center is temporarily closed. When the activity is finished, the student records which center was visited, cleans up, and moves to a new center. An example of a form to keep track of the centers a child visits can be found on page 49.

Learning Centers Record

Use this form for young learners.

Name _____ Start Date _____

The center I am working on is . . .   Color the face when you complete the center.

The center I am working on is . . .	Color the face when you complete the center.
1. _____ ------------------------------ _____	☺
2. _____ ------------------------------ _____	☺
3. _____ ------------------------------ _____	☺
4. _____ ------------------------------ _____	☺
5. _____ ------------------------------ _____	☺

A second way is to assign children to a group and dictate when and for how long the children are to attend a center. There are a variety of ways to rotate children through the centers. A couple of examples can be found on page 51.

If the children are to move from one center to another at a designated time, it is best if a standard signal, such as a bell, is used to tell children first to cleanup and then to move to the next center.

A third way is to assign children to groups and list the centers they are to attend that day on a work board (Fountas and Pinnell, 1996). There is no signal to move from one center to the next. The decision of when to move on is left up to the student. If the teacher schedules first, activities that are apt to take longer this method helps with the problem of unfinished work. A student is free to stay at the center until the activity is finished. Again, for accountability, a record of which centers were visited should be maintained by each student. In addition, there should be a couple of center choices for children who finish their lists before the end of guided reading time.

Usually four different lists of activities are sufficient for work boards. The following day, the list of groups is moved to the next list of activities. The lists can be changed at the teacher's discretion. In other words, the teacher can change the center when it is convenient to add variety or add a new activity after the children have been trained.

From past experience, grouping students heterogeneously reduces disruptions. This tends to minimize the disturbances that arise when one group contains all the struggling readers. In addition, it allows group makeup to be very flexible. The group members can be changed every four days. For guided reading, the children are pulled from their centers. They return to those centers (except perhaps for computer use, which is timed) when the guided reading group has finished.

This method can be modified so students can use individual contracts. In this case, the children could choose the order of activities, or the teacher could set the order with the work board.

From past experience, grouping students heterogeneously reduces disruptions.

Pocket Charts

Create a pocket chart, using colorful tagboard and library card pockets. Glue the pockets to the tagboard and laminate. Using a razor blade, cut a slit through the laminate at each pocket opening so the center cards will slide in easily.

With a permanent marker, write a student's name on each pocket. On index cards, draw a picture illustrating the center or write the name of each center. Make as many of each center card as the number of students allowed in that center at one time. (For example, if four students can use the science center at once, make four science cards.) Place the index cards in the pockets.

When you are ready to change centers, move the cards to the right. Be sure to space the cards so that students will not go to the same center two times in a row. (Don't put same-center cards next to each other.) You may wish to create a recordkeeping form so you know when each student has completed each center.

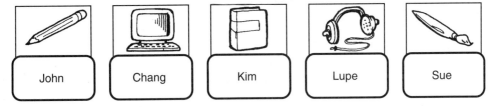

An alternate method is to purchase a pocket chart. In the top row of the pocket chart, place cards naming each group of students. Under each group name, place cards listing the centers. Sequence the centers so that only one group is working at a center at a time. When centers time begins, have students go to the first center listed in their group's column. When that center time is up, remove the top cards and have students go again to the top card in their column. Do this until you have completed the cycle of centers and the centers pockets are empty.

Red Group	Yellow Group	Green Group	Blue Group
Art	Science	Listening	Math
Math	Art	Science	Listening
Listening	Math	Art	Science
Science	Listening	Math	Art

Getting Started

Once you have decided how to rotate the children and which centers you are going to start with, you must teach the children how to work in centers. This includes expectations for behavior, how to use recording forms, cleanup, what to do when a center is temporarily closed, what to do with finished and unfinished work, signals for cleanup and rotation, how to resolve problems, what to do when help is needed, how to do the activities required at the different centers, how long they should stay at a center, and appropriate noise levels. It is important to get feedback from the children. Celebrate successes, discuss and resolve problems, and let the children know that they are doing a great job. This training process can take from four to six weeks.

> **Regardless of what type of activities the children do independently during guided reading time, it is worth the time and effort to train the children up front.**

Regardless of what type of activities the children do independently during guided reading time, it is worth the time and effort to train the children up front. Once the children are able to work independently, the teacher is free to concentrate on the guided reading group without worry, distractions, or interruptions. If children are not working independently, stop and retrain them.

Concluding Remarks

As teachers we do want to do what is best for children. Implementing a balanced program that includes guiding reading may seem intimidating. However, it is not necessary for you to throw your current program out the window. The whole point of guided reading, and by extension a balanced program, is that teachers control the program.

Evaluate your current program. Make a list of the different activities you have your children do. Honestly decide for each activity if it is effective (either educationally or managerially). If you drop an activity, decide which of these new ideas you could try. If you are starting a new program, look through this book and pick one thing that seems doable. Implement that first. As you become more confident, you will be ready to add more. You also will have had time to start working on collecting or making the materials you need to create your own balanced reading program.

The best thing about teaching is that it unleashes your creative talents. New ideas are a great catalyst. Use your experience and imagination to create a wonderful, effective reading program for your students!

Homework

Homework is the bane of most teachers—especially elementary teachers. However, this is one activity where parents expect to be involved. There are several areas that should be addressed. First, parents should understand the homework policy of the school or district. What the district expects may be more or less than the parent expects. Second, make homework somewhat flexible, especially for primary students. Children who have gymnastics, soccer practice, soccer games, and parents who spend almost every weekend four-wheeling in the desert, may not be able to do their four days of homework on Monday through Thursday. There may be more time on the weekend or on Mondays and Wednesdays. Third, make sure that the instructions for homework are clear. One way to accomplish this it to standardize the types of activities that are assigned for homework. Another suggestion is to make sure that homework is independent practice for the children. In other words, the children have already done a similar activity and practiced it under your supervision.

Finally, remember that asking children to read at home may be more difficult than you imagine. Most teachers grew up with books in their homes or weekly trips to the library. This is one of the reasons they loved school enough to want to go back as teachers. Not all children find themselves in this position. In addition, it is difficult to find books for beginning readers. Some publishers are beginning to address this, for example, *The Step-Up Books, The I Can Read* series, and the Barrons series, *Ready, Set, Go.* However, teachers have greater access to these low leveled books because they are published especially for schools. Many publishers now include take-home books with their materials. Some of these books are pre-printed, but usually they are distributed as blackline masters.

> Children who have gymnastics, soccer practice, soccer games, and parents who spend almost every weekend four-wheeling in the desert, may not be able to do their four days of homework on Monday through Thursday.

Unless you work at a dream school, your printing budget is probably limited. If it is not, by all means, copy and send home as many books as possible. For those of you who are not in dreamland, consider making four to six copies and asking the children to return the copies when they are tired of reading them. This way the children can take home books that are just the right level to practice reading and if a copy is lost, it will not break the bank to replace it. Book boxes (either cereal boxes cut in half or shoe boxes) that are decorated at school and then sent home provide places to keep these books. This externally imposed organization helps the child find these books when it is time to read. It also prevents the books from going A.W.O.L., never to be seen again.

Another successful strategy for getting the right books into the children's hands are book clubs. With an enthusiastic recommendation from the teacher, many parents are willing to spend a few dollars on books. Make sure parents know if the book is to be read aloud or if it is one the child can read independently. One particularly good series for independent reading is Scholastic's *Phonics Chapter Books*.

Planning and Organizing Guided Reading for Readers

What Is Guided Reading?

Guided reading is a structure that provides scaffolding. Scaffolding uses what students know and can do to access text that is beyond their abilities or experiences. As a structure it involves the interaction of several elements: the text, student, and teacher. It is within this structure that the teacher introduces concepts and strategies that help the student develop as a mature reader.

Often guided reading is used to target readers in the classroom who need support and additional help to engage themselves in and to understand the reading text.

Grouping

Most teachers group students for instruction one way or another. Grouping can be done to facilitate the delivery of initial instruction or to reteach. Children are commonly grouped by ability (homogeneously) or by mixed ability (heterogeneously).

The problem with homogeneous grouping is that students in the lower groups often lose out on valuable instruction that the more advanced groups receive. They also miss out on social exchanges with stronger students. If the grouping is static, the children quickly recognize what group they are in and begin to label themselves as smart or stupid.

Grouping should be based on the concepts to be taught, the materials necessary for the lesson, and the needs of the students. It should not be based solely upon the needs of the teacher or to make classroom management easier.

How Can Guided Reading Help My Students?

The primary purpose of guided reading is to allow the teacher to work with targeted students to enhance their reading experiences. Often guided reading is used to target in the classroom readers who need support and additional help to engage themselves in and to understand the reading text. Surely, this is where, as classroom teachers, we need to spend most of our time; however, guided reading is also an excellent tool to allow good or even exceptional readers to extend their reading experiences to a deeper level than they would achieve if left to their own devices. It has been our experience that without some guidance even good readers often read at a superficial level.

When the teacher is working with individuals or small groups of students, instruction can be more narrowly focused to serve their particular needs. Some possible instructional goals of guided reading follow:

Direct Focus During guided reading the teacher can help the students focus attention on the text. By using questioning and probing dialogue the teacher directs the students' attention. Directions might sound like this: "Look for..., Show your neighbor..., Place your bookmark on the last sentence of the first paragraph, Find the sentence that tells us..., Find the sentence that asks..., Fill in the word orally that I omit as I read aloud, Listen for words on our brainstorming list, Ask questions to yourself as you read the text."

Unknown Words Students' comprehension is often disrupted when they are confronted with difficult vocabulary or unknown words. To assist students, the teacher makes suggestions to help students develop strategies that will help the next time they run into this type of difficulty.

Provide Motivation Many students need help in establishing motives for reading. As students read the text either silently or orally, the teacher might trigger their curiosity (a powerful motivator) by asking them: Why has the protagonist faced this situation? Have you experienced a similar situation or know of someone who has? Why did the author write this book? In this case knowing the students is invaluable to help them make connections with the text and establish reasons for reading.

Encourage Imagination Guided reading provides an opportunity for the teacher to provoke students' imaginations. Students should always be encouraged to ask questions about the topics they are currently studying. At the same time they should be allowed autonomy to ponder and explore potential answers to those same questions. Not only does this provide motivation for student learning, it also encourages the use of their imaginations. Also, it is fair to say that most learning begins with some sort of a question like "I wonder why...?" It seems, at times, as if students have sometimes lost the ability to ask interesting questions about the world they live in by fourth grade (Duckworth, 1987).

True learning happens when an investigation or discovery is preceded by a question or an observation of a phenomenon that calls into question some previously held truth or belief. The question piques the student's curiosity.

Other questions to foster imagination include: Can you imagine yourself in this situation? Can you smell the flowers? What does the room look like? What words does the author use to help us to see these

> Students' comprehension is often disrupted when they are confronted with difficult vocabulary or unknown words.

scenes in our heads? During guided reading the teacher helps the students exercise and use their imaginations.

Provide Problem-Solving Opportunities Guided reading provides problem-solving practice. Every time a student is engaged intellectually with the text, he or she is faced with the same problems as the protagonist, or ponders why the heroine finds herself in such a terrible situation, or learns how to use something from the text to solve a similar problem. Do the characters' insights agree with the reader's previous understanding of how the world works, or is there some dissonance that will have to be resolved?

Several prompts for problem solving follow: How will he start a fire without matches? What are some ways he can find food? How will she find or build shelter in the desert? How would you solve this problem? Do you think this character will solve the problem the same way?

Increase Curiosity Often students have difficulty engaging themselves in a text because their curiosity is not aroused. Guided reading can help stimulate student curiosity by directing their attention to the title of the story, or the picture on the book jacket, or perhaps a discussion of the author and other books he or she has written.

Promote Understanding Meaning is the goal of reading! In a small group, the teacher can easily check student understanding.

Provoke Critical Thinking Comprehension happens only when the student reads critically. In guided reading the teacher helps students develop and use critical thinking skills through thought-provoking questions and probing.

Assist in Organization The ability to organize information supports reading comprehension and critical thinking. Organization of one's thoughts in the intermediate grades is very difficult. Students need many opportunities to gather information and to organize it in an accessible way. Through guided reading the teacher can help students improve their ability to organize and process information.

Develop Reading Maturity The ultimate goal of reading instruction is to lead students toward mature intellectual participation with the text. At this point, guided reading is no longer needed because the students have become their own reading "guides."

Whole Group, Small Group, or Individual Instruction

The goals of guided reading are, of course, the goals of a balanced program—to develop independent, mature, self-directed readers. Guided reading offers opportunities to work with an individual, a small group, or the entire class. A whole-class reading experience where every student is participating in the reading activity has advantages. Foremost

> Comprehension happens only when the student reads critically.

is that it is very efficient because the teacher is directly instructing each student.

However, whole-class instruction is one of the most difficult methods to master. No matter how well a whole-class lesson is designed, there are always a few students who are not engaged in the activity. They may be physically incapable of focusing for long periods of time, feel incompetent, habitually let their minds wander, or do something else because the subject does not interest them. These are the students who may benefit from small-group instruction.

How Do I Get Started?

Targeting Individual or Small Groups

First, determine which individuals or groups of students will benefit the most from small group instruction. Previous experience with the students will generally be enough to identify those students who do not engage in reading activities. Also consider students who never contribute to class discussions.

A reading record will help identify students who have not yet pulled together the strategies needed to read independently. If the teacher has not been trained to take reading records, taking notes as a child reads from a book that is leveled (even if it is just an approximate grade level) works just as well. Comprehension should be checked because there are some students who are able to correctly decode words but do not have the necessary background to make sense of the words.

> Comprehension should be checked because there are some students who are able to correctly decode words but do not have the necessary background to make sense of the words.

After reading a short text at an appropriate reading level, the student should be able to respond to factual questions that deal with setting, main characters, characterization, plot, and sequence of main events, as well as be able to identify the main problem and its resolution. Begin with questions that can be found in one sentence in the text. Ask questions so that the student must synthesize the answer from two or more locations. The most difficult questions are those that can not be taken directly from the text but are suggested by the text and inferred by the reader. These questions require the use of higher-level thinking skills.

Targeting the Whole Class

The teacher determines the reading objectives and provides the same guidance that he or she would in a small group. The advantage is that it is efficient when you want all students to participate with the same material, especially integrated themes about history or science. Another instance where whole-class instruction makes sense is when the text is not too difficult for most students, but the ideas are beyond their experience.

Structures

Guided reading can take several different forms, depending on the needs of the students, the teacher, and the teacher's resources.

Teacher-Driven Guided Reading

Probably the most common guided reading activity involves the teacher interacting with the students. They read orally or silently, depending on the learning objective. The teacher may work with an individual or a small group (six or less), depending on materials. The teacher sets the goals for the session, directs the activity, initiates discussion, asks questions, and probes for understanding.

Student-Driven Guided Reading

After modeling a guided reading activity, the teacher may wish to have students work in pairs. In this structure, the teacher and students decide on the objectives. The students then work together to accomplish these objectives. At the pre-arranged time, the teacher meets with the students to evaluate how well the students met the objectives and discuss, if appropriate, how the student session(s) went, what they accomplished, or what they want to change next time. This is a very powerful structure because it gives the responsibility for personal reading growth and autonomy to the students. In this type of reading experience, the teacher can expect failures as well as successes; however, gentle admonishment can be a successful tool to encourage students to take responsibility for their own learning in the future.

> The titles should include a large collection of nonfiction as well as fiction.

The teacher should think carefully about how he or she creates reading pairs. Personalities and reading abilities, along with the students' ability to work with others, are variables the teacher must consider. Two readers with similar abilities should be assigned material at their reading level. This allows them to concentrate on the objectives of the reading session. When the partners have differing abilities, a slightly more difficult text can be assigned to accommodate the better reader and challenge the other student.

Materials

The classroom should have a wide range of titles that are leveled over a wide range of reading ability—from primary to grade level and beyond in order to challenge good readers. The titles should include a large collection of nonfiction as well as fiction. Just as a classroom usually has a good selection of fiction genres, it should, too, have a selection of nonfiction genres such as biographies, autobiographies, personal experiences, opinions, essays, brochures, how to, science, math, history, and periodicals available. Selections of these materials should be accessible in any balanced reading program.

These materials should be available in sets of six or eight texts per title whenever possible. The Wright Group Sunshine Collection offers a wide range of fiction and nonfiction titles. These books are written in an easily digestible format. They are typically short, 30 to 40 pages, and have been leveled. Any favorite trade book, of course, can be purchased in sets of six. Do not overlook books that are sometimes mistakenly classified as primary books. *Ox-Cart Man* offers rich concepts which the relatively simple vocabulary and poetic form hide. Author Jean Fritz has written a series of biographies and other nonfiction books on the American Revolution that are also rich in concepts with fairly simple vocabulary. These books are well worth the investment of your discretionary classroom or other school reading funds.

Know Your Text

It seems a daunting task to familiarize yourself with every title. Even after several readings of a particular text, there are new discoveries to explore with students. It is important to think carefully about the students you will be working with, the reading objectives, student abilities and needs, and, of course, the text itself. Some texts lend themselves particularly well to specific goals such as characterization, or plot structure. For example, in *Ox-Cart Man,* students can explore the importance of the cyclic nature of life, consistency, and self-sufficiency on a colonial farm—heady content for fifth graders, much less the third graders to whom this wonderful book is often targeted.

Even after several readings of a particular text, there are new discoveries to explore with students.

How to Initiate Guided Reading

Shared Reading to Initiate Guided Reading

Guided reading is a natural extension of shared reading, whole-class reading, or independent reading activity. An explanation of these activities follows.

Shared reading is initiated by the teacher with the whole class. The selected text can be from any genre. It should be easily digested in a single sitting. A chapter from a longer text would also fit this requirement. The students' responsibilities are to listen to the text while keeping the objectives in mind. A follow-up activity may follow this session, depending on the learning objective. Usually, a text is shared over several sessions. During each session, the text is read aloud to the whole class. Subsequent readings may be done by a student reader. Each shared session is designed to meet a particular objective selected by the teacher. Activities may extend the reading.

Once the shared reading session has been concluded, including discussion, the class can be given directions for an activity. The teacher has several options for a small guided reading group. Each student has a copy of the text read during the shared reading. The teacher can have them reread the text orally or silently, after the teacher has given specific reading goals and support. The teacher may elect to have the targeted group work, with the teacher's support, on the same follow-up activity as the rest of the class with the teacher's support. This structure can be used after every shared reading event. Each time the teacher decides which students to include in the targeted group. This provides for dynamic student grouping.

Whole-Class Reading to Initiate Guided Reading

In a whole-class reading activity, everyone has a copy of the same text. Presumably, this will be core literature, a selection from the reading series, or another textbook. For chapter books, each chapter can be treated like a short book.

A novel matrix is a good way to record a retelling, event sequence, new characters, or changes that the main character goes through as conflicts are resolved, as well as new vocabulary and predictions.

It may be helpful to do plot map and record how the readers' concerns vary with each new obstacle that the protagonist faces.

After each chapter the teacher can initiate guided reading with a targeted group of students. This allows the teacher to ensure the students are able to keep up with the reading and that they will be able to complete the extended activity.

Independent Reading to Initiate Guided Reading

Independent reading time is a structure during which each child is reading a text of his or her choice. It is sometimes called Reading Workshop. In Reading Workshop, the session often begins with a ten to fifteen minute "mini-lesson" on a selected reading topic designed for the whole class. After the "mini-lesson" the students read from texts they select. Usually there is some predetermined criteria that the students need to meet in selecting a text. This could be a particular genre or from a predetermined list of books. The students keep logs of their reading accomplishments for the year. For an example of a reading log, refer to page 61. As the students begin to read, the teacher moves from student to student to discuss the text and give prompts for strategies as necessary. The teacher keeps his or her own log, recording the students' reading progress. These notes provide the source and inspiration for the next "mini-lesson."

This time can also be used for a small-group guided reading session. In this case, the students would be working with texts of their choice or the teacher's choice.

Independent reading time is a structure during which each child is reading a text of his or her choice.

This is a blank copy of the same form that was demonstrated on page 37. It can be duplicated for students to use as a part of their own record keeping.

Student Reading Record
UPPER GRADE

Name: _____

Date	Title of Book	# of pages	Response to Book (written or oral report, other)

What Does the Class Look Like?

There are several things going on at the same time, either a whole class activity, individual projects, or center activities with a small-group meeting with the teacher. Each activity has been pre-orchestrated by the teacher. Standards for behavior and the activities that students are presently engaged in have been carefully planned. Each student knows to move on to the next activity when the current activity is finished. Students know where to get supplies, how to record their efforts, and how to file their products without consulting the teacher. Classroom procedures for use of the restrooms, movement about the classroom, and talking with other students are well established. Most routine problems are handled by the students themselves with the help of classroom officers.

If students feel they must discuss an issue with the teacher before proceeding, they know to work on another activity until the teacher is no longer engaged with a small group. An ideal classroom? Yes. Can a classroom really function like this? Yes. Does it always function like this 100 percent of the time without adjustment, restating standards, or classroom meetings to discuss problem issues? No.

These are issues that are worked out at the beginning of the school year and revisited during the school year as necessary. If the classroom can function on its own, then the students are functioning on their own, and they are accepting responsibility for their own learning.

During a small guided reading group, it will be necessary to monitor the classroom to ensure that students are on task and are busily engaged in some activity. Usually a visual check is sufficient. The noise level and type of conversation is also a good indicator that students are following classroom standards and procedures. The classroom teacher, of course, needs to plan how to handle interruptions. Usually eye contact, a word to a classroom officer, saying the student's name aloud, or changing the student's seating will suffice.

What Will the Other Students Be Doing?

After a reading activity, i.e., shared, independent, or whole class, the teacher may choose to extend the text by assigning a language arts activity or investigation for students to work on individually or in small groups.

There are an endless number of activities and investigations that are beneficial to young readers. There are many things to consider before jumping headlong into any activity. First, there are the practical limitations. How much preparation time will this activity take? Do I have the necessary resources to do this activity? How much time will it take in the classroom? How will materials be handled? Equally important, consider if the activity is consistent with your philosophy of learning. What direct benefit will the children receive from the activity? Is the amount of time spent on the activity worth the return in increased reading ability?

To explore and extend a particular book, the students might complete activities designed around story structure by studying the literary elements such as characters, setting, plot, theme, mood and tone, point of view or voice, and symbolism (Roll, 1996).

Centers and Long-Term Projects As mentioned earlier many classrooms are organized around centers. These might include math, language arts, science, and history. These activities are usually designed so students follow certain procedures to get materials, check, record, and report their efforts. For example, Marcy Cook Math Tiles are designed to be used in centers. The materials, procedures, checking, tracking, and recording are all included. Most teachers are able to modify other materials to work as a center. A great deal of time and effort as well as trial and error are required to design a classroom built around centers. However, once the teacher has gained this competency, the results are well worth the effort.

An excellent format for long-term projects is called "I-Search."

Long-term projects in language arts, history, and science are also valuable activities students can work on as time becomes available. It helps to prevent the student asking, "What should I do now?" Science, health, geography, and history offer a rich background for long-term project topics. It is important to offer choices when students choose a topic to study. The project requirements and the criteria for grading or the rubric need to be carefully thought out before introducing the project.

An excellent format for long-term projects is called "I-Search." This format guides the student through the various phases of a report. It also fits well into a constructivist philosophy. It asks the student to consider first what is already known about the topic, what he or she wants to learn about the topic, the successes and failures along the way, and, finally, what was learned. Notice the importance of questioning at the beginning phases of the project before the student begins his or her research. It is the questioning that motivates and guides the student in his or her efforts.

The project is usually divided into three products: a written report, a poster, and an oral presentation. The poster offers students an opportunity to summarize their knowledge into three or four key ideas and present these in a visual format. The poster also serves as a visual aid for the oral report. The oral report offers students the opportunity to establish themselves as experts about the topic.

During the oral presentations the class practices their listening and note-taking skills. Students also discuss the merits of all the products of each project. After digesting all the projects about a subject, students are given an opportunity to compare and contrast the reports and come up with generalizations about the topic.

Vocabulary Memory Game This vocabulary activity is a variation on the memory game. Here groups of four students divide up the text and search out new or questionable vocabulary words. Each vocabulary word is written on a card 3" x 5" (8 cm x 15 cm), and the definition written on another card. The students share with each other the words (or a percentage of them) with their group so that they can become familiar with the words. Working in groups of twos, the students compete with each other to attempt to match up as many words with their definitions as possible.

Name the Character In this game the students search for the physical attributes of the characters in a story. Cards can be used to record the characters' names and attributes. The students read one attribute at a time while the other team attempts to guess the character. Points can be awarded, and students can challenge each team to verify their clues. A more difficult game can be played by listing character attributes such as honesty or sloth. By playing charades students can act out one of the characters while the others guess who it is.

Reenactments Small groups of students can reenact the chapter or book, focusing on how to distinctly portray each character. Costuming and makeup can be added. This is, of course, a very engaging and exciting activity. Behavior standards will have to be set and closely monitored. Consider videotaping the presentations. These tapes can be used to share student work with parents (almost every household owns a VCR) or as part of Open House.

Puppets A story with strong characters can be reenacted with a set of simple paper-doll puppets constructed from light cardboard or construction paper and taped to rulers. Make sure the students practice before they perform for the class. Do not forget the importance of students evaluating each other's efforts. Were they true to their characters and the story? For more information about dramatization, refer to pages 46 and 47.

Where Am I? This is a guessing game that might be used in a chapter book with several settings. The students formulate yes/no questions to determine the clues they need to correctly identify the setting.

Drawing the Setting Students draw the setting based upon the description or inferences from the book.

Small groups of students can reenact the chapter or book, focusing on how to distinctly portray each character.

64

Writing Activities Another way for students to extend their exploration of a text is through writing. Most of the preceding activities require students to record observations, write summaries, write reports, list and classify words, etc. Once students have explored a particular genre and have identified its characteristics, they can (with the teacher's help) create a "recipe" for the genre. Then they can write original stories using this "recipe." Students can also record their thoughts and observations about literature in journals as they read through a text. Another possibility is to write an innovation, sequel, or different ending for a given text (McCracken and McCracken, 1988).

Graphic Organizers Students can also explore story genres, compare books by the same author, and study similar themes in different books using story or genre matrices. Matrices are very flexible and can take many forms. They can be very simple or extremely complex, depending on the needs of the class. Matrices are helpful because they help students focus on a topic or interest. A matrix is just one type of graphic organizer. Venn diagrams, charts, tables, outlines, webs, and time lines are also useful. A mind map is another useful device that presents a visual picture of story elements and their relationship to each other. Mind maps provide an opportunity for visually/spatially intelligent students to shine. Plot maps show the relationships among the initial event, subsequent events, the rising level of concern as the reader responds to the events, the climax, its resolution, and denouement. Teacher Created Materials' *Activities for Any Literature Unit: Intermediate* has generic work sheets, games, art activities, and teaching ideas that are ideal for extending any text.

Of course none of these tools can be used by the students without instruction, guided practice, and feedback.

Of course none of these tools can be used by the students without instruction, guided practice, and feedback. Once students become familiar with several extending activities, their use is unlimited and not just for literature but science and social studies as well. While most of these ideas for extending a text can be done by a whole class, they can also be adapted for small groups.

What Kinds of Activities Will I Be Doing with My Small Group?

In the whole-class environment, students have read and explored a text as a classroom experience. They are working on an extended activity or some other activity within the classroom. As a classroom teacher you feel satisfied that the class is working independently. You want to work with a small group of readers, perhaps, to check what they got from the recently completed reading activity or to give them support in completing the current classroom activity, or, perhaps, to reteach some component of literacy. All these are excellent options. First,

First, determine which students you will be targeting during the guided reading session: (1) the students who are struggling readers, (2) advanced readers, (3) a group of mixed ability students, or (4) a group of non-English or limited-English speaking students.

Guided Reading for Struggling Readers

It will be helpful to think about the attributes of good readers as we consider how to best work with struggling readers.

Good readers engage themselves intellectually with the text. They begin to anticipate the contents and the subsequent actions of the book. The anticipation is an intellectual perception which is built when children ask themselves questions and make predictions and inferences about the contents. This is the foundation laid down by readers with which they begin the book and continue to build on throughout the reading experience. The degree to which they are able to accomplish this is limited by the extent of their reading experience.

Good readers engage themselves intellectually with the text.

Good readers approach a text with expectation and confidence in themselves as readers.

Without a consciousness of effort, good readers use their knowledge about the structure of the printed word, the sound/symbol relationship, phonics, the flow of the print, knowledge of story line, recognition of story genre, grammatical patterns, story structure, etc., to extract meaning from the text. This is done as an integrated and relatively seamless intellectual assault on the text. The degree to which this assault is seamless depends again on their experience as readers. An unexplored story structure or a topic requiring prior knowledge might cause the reader to be tentative.

- Good readers read for longer periods of time and read more complex books. They read a wide range of books, including fiction, poetry, and nonfiction. Good readers read to be informed and for personal enjoyment.

- Good readers also have a working understanding of the literary elements of the text, such as setting, characterization, plot, and theme.

- Good readers can summarize and retell stories and communicate with others about the story.

- Good readers are able to identify and discuss the author's purpose in writing the book.

- When reading out loud good readers read fluently and with expression.

If these attributes represent good readers, then struggling readers must be deficient, or at least partially deficient, in one or more of these. Just as we come to expect good readers' efforts to be somewhat integrated and seamless, so, too, deficiencies in reading ripple across the spectrum of what we come to think of as reading skills.

It is very difficult if not impossible for a classroom teacher to isolate, pinpoint, and teach each deficiency of a given child within the context of a classroom of 30 or more students. Even if a teacher could efficiently isolate and pinpoint a deficient reading skill and then provide remediation, that same teacher would then be faced with the task of rediagnosing to isolate and prescribe instruction for the next deficiency until at some point in the school year, this hypothetically deficient reader was reading and comprehending at the expected level.

The problem is that the classroom teacher is trying to isolate one component of literacy from the whole as if reading were just a series of isolated components strung one after another in a line that stretches out until at the end, like a fish on a hook, the literate person is reached.

This part-whole approach is not real-life literacy. How, then, can we identify the deficiencies and guide students towards true literacy? One important step is to help students recognize when they come to a problem. The teacher can then note the difficulty and later help the student develop strategies that will solve the problem next time it arises.

> How, then, can we identify the deficiencies and guide students towards true literacy?

Students learn best when they begin with a complete unit of meaning, that is, the whole text itself. Once students have grasped a general sense of the text, it can be broken down into meaningful parts.

It does little good to spend a great deal of time of trying to sound out a single word. The knowledge of a single word will not be transferred to a related word unless children learn to recognize patterns and repeated structures within words and stories.

So then, what are we to do with our small reading group of struggling readers? Since literacy is directly related to the readers' experiences, we simply give them many opportunities to read with just enough support so the students can work through the difficulties. In other words, we guide the students through the reading of the text. Additionally, we look for teaching opportunities in the text. However, too much teaching interrupts the flow and continuity of the story and obscures the meaning. Guided reading offers the scaffolding necessary to aid young readers until they mature and gain the confidence necessary to read independently.

There are some characteristics of a supportive classroom environment that are worthy of consideration.

- The teacher is supportive of student efforts.
- Mistakes are considered a natural part of the learning cycle. The teacher respects the students' efforts.

- Most of the activities the children are engaged in should be considered as opportunities to practice and explore the use of language. Their efforts should not be thought of as opportunities to give grades. Grades are permanent, and they label the child's practice as worthy or unworthy. It is the support, praise, and feedback about their efforts that is important.
- The classroom provides many opportunities to practice listening, speaking, reading, and writing.
- The teacher should be a dynamic influence in the classroom.
- The teacher constantly encourages students to make an effort and complete activities.
- The classroom activities are designed in such a way that all students experience success.

Guided Reading for Strong Readers

Strong readers need support to extend their experiences with more varied and complex literature in the same way as struggling readers. The activities and investigations take the same format. The teacher's role, again, is to guide the students through the text. The vocabulary and the concepts will be more difficult and more challenging than they have yet experienced. The structure or form of the text may be new. In a sense, as strong readers extend their reading experiences, it is their turn to struggle.

Advanced readers are not only adept at the skills required of good readers, they usually have excellent critical thinking skills. However, they need to continue to develop or become aware of these skills, to understand the author's intent behind the story, and to think about character motivation and themes. They need to continue to ask themselves how this reading experience helps them to understand how other people live, how the characters struggle to make sense of the world in which they live, and how they reconcile their lives to it.

Guided Reading for Mixed Groups

Struggling readers need opportunites to work with good readers. Reading does not take place in a social vacuum. As readers interact, the social interchange supports all readers. Every student benefits from the experiences and insights of the others. The mixing of students also helps to avoid labeling students.

Guided Reading for Second Language Learners

A small-group structure can benefit second language learners. Second language learners need a great deal of support and encouragement within the classroom. The small group with teacher support can pro-

> Strong readers need support to extend their experiences with more varied and complex literature in the same way as struggling readers.

vide a secure environment which encourages students to experiment, make mistakes without ridicule, develop vocabulary, and learn to use language in meaningful situations.

Working with second language learners requires forethought and careful planning to create learning situations that we sometimes take for granted because of the rich background and experience that English language learners bring to the classroom. A lesson delivered to a whole class that is rich with give and take between students and teacher, full of hands-on materials, word lists, mind maps, KWL charts, social interactions among students, note-taking, and humor can present a confusing and chaotic picture to a non-English or limited-English speaking student.

Guided reading guides the learner through the reading material in such a way as to provide support and instruction to ensure comprehension. At the same time, the teacher looks for opportunities to help the reader become a fully functioning, mature, and independent reader. The teaching points are chosen and timed so they do not sacrifice or interfere with meaning. After all, it is the meaning of what we read that enriches our lives.

For students learning English, the teacher must mediate to provide the background needed to comprehend the text. Issues such as lack of knowledge of the American culture, loneliness, shyness, awkwardness, and the dizzying shock that children feel when confronted with new and strange situations must also be taken into consideration when planning lessons.

Much of the social awkwardness can not be averted, but teachers ease the transition to English with patience and attention to the special needs of these students. A small group offers second language learners opportunities to observe, speak, read, and write in a controlled environment. It can also focus on the strengths that these students bring with them from their own rich cultures. In the safe environment of a small mixed group, students learn from each other and exchange information about their cultures. This is also a wonderful opportunity for the teacher to become a learner.

Using Guided Reading in the Content Areas

A survey of books in the classroom would generally show that the number of fictional texts far outnumber the number of nonfiction texts. In general, the recommended core literature and classroom book sets again are overwhelmingly fiction. Even the material in classroom anthologies is mostly fiction. Yet a visit to the local library shows that the majority of books there are nonfiction. While fiction provides a source of diversion and gives us insight into the human condition, it is in nonfiction that there are explanations of how the

> A lesson delivered to a whole class that is rich with give and take between students and teacher, full of hands-on materials, word lists, mind maps, KWL charts, social interactions between students, note-taking, and humor can present a confusing and chaotic picture to a non-English or limited-English speaking student.

world works, self-help, self-improvement, hobbies, income opportunities, and perhaps, job advancement.

Indeed, as students progress through school, textbooks that present factual information far exceed fictional texts. Beginning early in elementary school, the first books that children come in contact with are storybooks. Very quickly, though, more and more of the information that students need comes from mathematics, history, health, grammar, and skill books.

This is an area where struggling readers and sometimes even good readers often have difficulty. Most reading instruction is based on understanding story structure and the storywriter's conventions. It is not surprising then that readers struggle with expository text.

There are many different kinds of textbooks, and each type has its own structure. When students try to use multiple resources during research, texts may contradict each other. Experts in a particular field may not be experts in children's books. A text may present a confusing array of charts, graphs, vocabulary full of confusing technical terms, and concepts that are outside the experiences of young readers.

Even with these negatives, children are highly motivated to read nonfiction—just like adults. They love to read about unusual animals and collect interesting and bizarre bits of information. They love to read and study about their favorite sports heroes. They often study technical manuals to learn how something works. Children even subscribe to specialized magazines to learn about their hobbies or to learn strategies for playing video games.

In a classroom environment the decision of what to read is usually determined by the school district, state curriculum frameworks, and the classroom teacher. Children have little choice in what they study, so they often do not buy into the lessons. When you tap into their interests and presenting nonfiction texts, the students are motivated, they learn how to read nonfiction, and finally, they are able to store their knowledge and background about how the world works.

The requirements for a guided reading lesson for nonfiction are the same for individuals, small groups, or whole groups. The teacher helps the readers, page by page, through the book to get the author's meaning. The reading is uninterrupted. The teacher skillfully questions and probes the students to make sure they are comprehending what they are reading. The special skills that are necessary to function independently as a mature nonfiction reader are taught in context. As in all learning activities, the teacher first models the skill, encourages the students to practice the skill with support, and then allows the students to independently put the skill to use.

> **It is not surprising then that readers struggle with expository text.**

Generating Reading Motivation

For some students, it is not sufficient to simply ask them to read a chapter without providing a motivation to read. Students can be motivated through the use of questioning to stimulate interest and curiosity, by previewing the topic, accessing prior knowledge, and suggesting the benefits of new learning.

Questioning Questions that motivate students can be deceptively simple. For example, if the class is going to study water, the question could be as simple as, "What do we know about water?" The answers are then recorded on a KWL chart. Questioning does many things. It may activate prior knowledge. Students use this prior knowledge about a subject as a framework for assimilating in new material. Questions can also be used to focus and direct student efforts toward specific goals, such as "What kinds of things can we learn about water?" The exchange of questions and responses encourages the students to anticipate what they might learn from their reading. Anticipation is an important motivational factor in learning (McCracken and McCracken, 1990).

Previewing A teacher can draw the students' attention to the chapter title and subtitles. Perhaps they read the first page together or other passages that hint at what is in the chapter. The students are directed to examine the pictures, photographs, graphs, charts, and captions. Collaboratively, the students and teacher make observations and comments as they progress through the text. The teacher may want to document questions as they arise.

Finally, a teacher's positive influence motivates students by guaranteeing success, providing clear information, feedback, and encouragement as the students work through roadblocks.

Students Need Help Finding Information

Teachers also need to guide students in learning how to find information. Some students must be taught how to skim through a text in search for specific information. They may need to be taught how to look up passages or read a complete text to make generalizations. Students may need to be shown how to use the index, the table of contents, or an appendix to find specific information. They may need help understanding the structure in which the content is presented: description, narrative, comparison and contrast, sequence, cause and effect, or problem solution. Additionally, students may need help understanding the purpose of the text, such as informative, persuasive, or entertaining.

> A teacher's positive influence motivates students by guaranteeing success, providing clear information, feedback, and encouragement as the students work through roadblocks.

Students Need Help Processing Information

Children do not automatically reflect on the material they read. In order for students to process information, they must anticipate what can be learned and bring together their prior knowledge with the information presented in the text. Teachers need to assist students when their background knowledge is not sufficient to process the new information.

Brian Cutting (1992) offers several ways that children can process content. With help students can make a list of the things they read about. They can use comparing and contrasting, cause and effect, similarities and differences, and problems and solutions recorded on a variety of charts to help them organize information. Students can take notes and later expand on the ideas in a reflective journal. Students can look for the main idea and the details that support it.

Students Need to Use Information

Students value learning when they have opportunities to share with others. When students become experts in different subjects, they are excited to learn and to share this knowledge with others. Learning should not happen in a vacuum. Written reports and writing books are popular ways that children share what they have learned. Reports can be presented in a variety of ways, including oral reports, posters, and computer multimedia presentations.

Concluding Remarks

Learning to read is a complex task. There is no way to guarantee that all children will learn at the same rate or with the same methods. There will always be students who need additional support to continue to expand their reading abilities. Guided reading offers an efficient way to guide these students on their journeys as successful learners.

Students value learning when they have opportunities to share with others.

References

Adams, M. J. (1990). <u>Beginning to read: Thinking and learning about print</u>. Cambridge, MA: M.I.T. Press.

Avery, C. (1993). <u>And with a light touch: Learning about reading, writing, and teaching with first graders</u>. Portsmouth, NH: Heinemann.

Banks, L.R. (1980). <u>The Indian in the cupboard</u>. NY: Avon Books.

Bear, D. R., Invernizzi, M., Templeton, S., and Johnston, F. (1996). <u>Words their way: Word study for phonics, vocabulary, and spelling instruction</u>. Columbus, OH: Merrill.

Cambourne, Brian, (1988). <u>The whole story: Natural learning and the acquisition of literacy in the classroom</u>. Auckland, New Zealand: Ashton Scholastic.

Clay, M. M. (1991). <u>Becoming literate: The construction of inner control</u>. Portsmouth, NH: Heinemann.

Clay, M. M. (1993). <u>An observation survey of early literacy achievement</u>. Portsmouth, NH: Heinemann.

Cunningham, P. M. (1995). <u>Phonics they use: Words for reading and writing</u>. NY: HarperCollins.

Cunningham, P. M. and Allington, R. L. (1994). <u>Classrooms that work: They can all read and write</u>. NY: Longman.

Cunningham, P. M. and Allington, R. L. (1999). <u>Classrooms that work: They can all read and write</u>. NY: Longman.

Cunningham, P. M., Hall, D. P., and Defee, M. (1998). <u>Nonability-grouped, multilevel instruction: eight years later</u>. Reading Teacher, 51, 652–664.

Cutting, B. (1992). <u>Moving on in whole language</u>. Bothell, WA: The Wright Group.

Dole, Duffy, Roehler, and Pearson. (1991). <u>Moving from the old to the new: Research on reading comprehension instruction</u>. Review of Educational Research, 61, 239–264.

Duckworth, E.R. (1987). "The having of wonderful ideas" and other essays on teaching and learning. NY: Teachers College Press.

Fountas, I. C. and Pinnell, G. S. (1996). Guided reading: Good first teaching for all children. Portsmouth, NH: Heinemann.

Ginsburg, M. (1972). The chick and the duckling. NY: Macmillan.

Juel, C. (1988). Learning to Read and Write: A Longitudinal Study of Fifty-Four Children from First Through Fourth Grade. Journal of Education Psychology, 80, 437–447.

Kunhardt, E. (1987). Step into reading: Pompeii . . . buried alive! NY: Random House.

McCracken, R. A. and McCracken, M. J. (1990). Survival handbook: Teaching reading through literature in the intermediate grades. British Columbia, Canada: McCracken Educational Services, Inc.

McCracken, M. J. and McCracken, R. A. (1995). Reading, writing and language: A practical guide for primary teachers. Manitoba, Canada: Peguis Publishers.

McCracken, R. and McCracken, M. (1988). Songs, stories and poetry to teach reading and writing. Manitoba, Canada: Peguis Publishers.

McCracken, R. and McCracken, M. (1991). Where do you live? Tiger cub books. Manitoba, Canada: Peguis Publishers.

Roll, D. (Ed.) (1996). Sunshine levels 6–11 teacher guide. Bothell, WA: The Wright Group.

Stanovich, K. E. (1986). Matthew effects in reading: Some consequences of individual differences in the acquisition of literacy. Reading Research Quarterly, 21, 360–407.

Wylie, R. E. and Durrell, D. D. (1970). Elementary English, 47, 787–791.

Trumbauer, L. (1998). Animals hide. NY: Newbridge Educational Publishing.

Veatch, J. (1959). Individualizing your reading program. New York: Putnam.

Additional References

Bond, G. L., and Dykstra, R. (1967). The cooperative research program in first-grade reading instruction. Reading Research Quarterly, 2, 5–142.

Clay, M. M. (1985). The early detection of reading difficulties. Auckland, New Zealand: Heinemann Education.

Gentry, R. (1981). Learning to spell developmentally. Reading Teacher, 34, 378-381.

Hall, D., Prevette, C., and Cunningham, P. (1995). Eliminating ability grouping and failure in the primary grades. In R. L. Allington & S. A. Walmsley (Eds.) No quick fix; Rethinking literacy programs in America's elementary schools. NY: Teachers College Press.

Holdaway, D. (1979). The foundations of literacy. Sydney, Australia: Ashton Scholastic.

Holdaway, D. (1990). Independence in reading: A handbook on individualized procedures. Sydney, Australia: Ashton Scholastic.

Hoskisson, K. and Tompkins, G. E. (1987). Language arts: Content and teaching strategies. Columbus, OH: Merrill Publishing Company.

Johnston, P. A. and Allington, R. L. (1991). Remediation. In Barr, R., Kamil, M., Mosenthal, P., and Pearson, P. D. (Eds.) Handbook of Reading Research, vol. w, (pp. 984–1012). New York: Longman.

Moore, D. W., Readence, J. E., and Rickelman, R. J. (1989). Prereading activities for content area reading and learning. Newark DE: International Reading Association.

Teacher Created Materials Resource List

TCM 147 Activities for any Literature Unit: Primary

TCM 266 Apples

TCM 2037 How to Manage Learning Centers in the Classroom

TCM 2421 Integrating Technology into the Language Arts Curriculum

TCM 619 Native American Arts and Cultures

TCM 891 Learning Centers

TCM 2316 Phonics, Phonemic Awareness Word Recognition Activities

TCM 2009 Writing Workshop: Lessons and Activities for the Writing Process